YES WE CAN

YES WE CAN

A BIOGRAPHY OF
BARACK OBAMA

Garen Thomas

FEIWEL AND FRIENDS

New York

A FEIWEL AND FRIENDS BOOK
An Imprint of Macmillan

Library of Congress Cataloging-in-Publication Data

Thomas, Garen Eileen.
Yes we can: a biography of Barack Obama / by Garen
Thomas.
p.   cm.
ISBN-13: 978-0-312-53709-8 / ISBN-10: 0-312-53709-3
1. Obama, Barack.   2. African Americans—
Biography.   3. African American legislators—
Biography.   4. Legislators—United
States—Biography.   5. United States. Congress. Senate—
Biography.   6. Presidential candidates—United States—
Biography.   7. Racially mixed people—United
States—Biography.   I. Title.
E901.1.O23T46 2008
328.73092—dc22
[B] 2008015316

BOOK DESIGN BY AMANDA DEWEY

Feiwel and Friends logo designed by Filomena Tuosto

First Edition: July 2008

1   3   5   7   9   10   8   6   4   2

www.feiwelandfriends.com

ACKNOWLEDGMENTS

I would like to thank my editors at Feiwel and Friends, Jean Feiwel and especially Liz Szabla, for giving me the flexibility to write this story from a perspective not often seen in children's books. I appreciate your faith in my vision and ability to carry it out from start to finish. Martin Baldessari worked nonstop to locate and get permission for the array of images you see here. Thanks to Rich Deas and the design team for an amazing layout and cover, which capture the spirit of this work beyond anything I could have imagined. I am grateful to Professor Ronald Loui, for all his effort and support as I slogged through this process, and to Bernice Bowers, for her kind contribution. Thank you to Gabby, Dave, and Holly for keeping me on track.

I would like to dedicate this work to my parents, who always believed I could. And to Zuri, whom I know also can.

CONTENTS

PROLOGUE

Many of you reading this work have only known one person in your lifetime to have held the position of president of the United States of America. The president can only serve a total of eight years in office (four in his first term, plus four in his second). The current president is serving his eighth year and cannot run again. Therefore, it is time for a change. Change, in this case, is inevitable.

But sometimes people have to take it upon themselves to make a difference and make change happen. One of the most exciting things about this current election is that the United States is going to make history, when the Democratic Party chooses either a man of color or a woman to represent it in the race for the White House. That has never happened before in our union. That is the definition of change—and what many would call progress.

As this election cycle began, I did not know whom to support. All I knew was that as the days passed, each issue our country was facing—the faltering economy, global warming and the erosion of the natural world, the loss of military and civilian lives in the unending war in Iraq— seemed to grow more and more urgent, while our government seemed to offer fewer and fewer solutions. The good thing about a democracy is that the voters have the right to change who is running the government when it isn't running well—when it is in need of an overhaul.

People of my parents' generation seemed to have lost some hope for a better future, having experienced the negative ways this country has treated many of its own. I am their immediate descendant, so I remain closely tied to that reality. It is difficult for me to tuck my parents' pain away when I recognize how many people, including people in government, have tried to silence the leaders of their generation—leaders who had given them hope.

There has emerged a new leader who seems to be granting Americans a renewed license to dream. Barack Obama has proven repeatedly that he can touch people from all genders, political affiliations, and across racial divides. What people find unique about this candidate is that he has managed to move those of my generation, as well as people from yours and my parents'. Perhaps this is because his caregivers came from different continents, different generations, different religions, different incomes, and different ethnic identities. People believe he understands them, because by some measure he is them and has cared deeply for individuals just like them. He manages, through what appears to be genuine concern, to uplift those who have fallen and bring hope anew to both the cynic and the idealist.

It is encouraging that you, the next generations, have taken an interest in this election, and seem to be hoping for a less predictable outcome. Your optimism, despite all the world's crises, is increasing. You see hope for the future, which has amazed the rest of us and sparked many of us to work with you toward that goal, that change.

There are few times in your life when you have a real opportunity to alter the course of history and put civilization back on a course toward prosperity and unity for all races and genders. If you were to look at dates in your history books, you might see centuries pass before something remarkable and worth noting occurred, when one person or a group of people stood up for change, making an enlightened leap in the evolution of the human story.

I hope, for the sake of the optimism you carry so boldly in your open palms, the time for that next leap is now, for hope can be as fragile and fleeting as a snowflake. Whoever the next president turns out to be, and however he—or she—toils to right past wrongs, making the country a little more free, a little more equal for all, know that you always have the power and voice and responsibility to push for more progress and insist on change in order to protect the dreams of your children . . . and elders.

You have changed me.

Obama Family Tree

Sarah ("Granny")
(Hussein's third wife)

Omar Zeituni Yusuf Sayed

HUSSEIN ONYANGO OBAMA — AKUMU
1895–1979   *1895–unknown*
                                 (Hussein's
                                 second wife)

Helima
(Hussein's first wife)

Sarah   Auma

Kezia —————— BARACK HUSSEIN OBAMA, SR.
(Barack Sr.'s first wife)   *1936–1982*

Abongo ("Roy"),
Auma, Abo,
Bernard

Ruth
(Barack Sr.'s third wife)

                                 BARACK HUSSEIN
                                 b. 1961

Mark David

Name unkown
(mother of George)

George

STANLEY "GRAMPS"
ARMOUR DUNHAM —— MADELYN "TOOT" LEE PAYNE
1918–1992 *b. 1922*

STANLEY ANN DUNHAM —— Lolo Soetoro
(Barack Sr.'s second wife) (Stanley Ann's second husband)
1942–1995 *1936–1987*

Maya Kassandra Soetoro
(Barack Jr.'s half sister)
b. 1970

OBAMA, JR. —— **MICHELLE LAVAUGHN ROBINSON**
b. 1964

Malia Natasha
b. 1999 *b. 2001*

YES WE CAN

"In the **end**, that is
          God's greatest gift
to us . . .
          a belief in things
                    not seen. . . ."[1]

His father was a legend, like John Henry:

strong, determined, larger than life. And as with all legends, the line between reality and fiction—that which is true and not true—got blurred over time. Was Barack Obama, Sr., really the grown man who had lifted his friend high over his head, pretending he was going to drop him over a cliff because his friend had accidentally dropped his pipe?

Did Barack Obama, Sr., actually stand up to a man in a bar who had refused to be served alongside black people? Is it a fact that he lectured the bigoted man on the dangers of racism and the sickness of segregation (keeping people of different races separate), leaving the man so ashamed of himself that he offered Obama $100 to buy his forgiveness?

Had Kenyan leaders and American sponsors really selected Barack Obama, Sr., to be educated in the United States so he could bring back new information and technologies to help modernize Kenya?

Barack Obama, the boy, did not get to know his father, Barack Obama, the man, in life. Except for a brief meeting when he was ten, all the younger Barack had of his father were imprints his dad had left behind with others: images on photographic paper and memories burned inside the minds of those who had known him. Could Barack *believe* in a man he remembered seeing only once?

With little more than other people's memories of his father to go on, Barack Obama did not feel completely whole. He knew just one of his parents and, as much as his mother tried, she couldn't give him all the knowledge he needed to become a man. There were other male figures in his life— his grandfather, his stepfather, an older black poet—but which of them was he supposed to emulate? His mother was white, but Barack could not ignore the fact that he was black, even when he didn't feel like a member of that community. Race in America has always been defined less by where you come from (or from whom), and more by that drop of blood you got from somewhere else, and by what you look like to people who don't even know you. Barack Obama looked black. His mother told him that he got his eyebrows from her, but his wit and character came from his father, as did so many of his other features: his nose; his cheeks and smile; his hair texture; his long; lean body; the ginger color of his skin, which was like a swirl of milk in coffee.

His mother's family didn't assign Barack a race—to them, he was family, pure and simple. But the rest of the world saw Barack differently. So how could Barack Obama, the innocent boy, learn to become Barack Obama, the grown black man, when the one person who could teach him was no longer part of his family? When the stories of the man who gave him his outward image were as believable as a fairy tale? Little did Barack know that most of the tales of his father were true, and though other tales had been stretched so thin they had snapped, his childhood would mirror his dad's in many, many ways. And Barack's search for the truth behind the legend of his father would lead him to a self-awareness and understanding of others that would define him as a leader.

"The road we have taken
to this point
has not been easy.
But, then again,
the road to change never is."[2]

Barack Hussein Obama, Sr., met Stanley

Ann Dunham at the University of Hawaii in Manoa in 1960. He had been born into the Luo tribe in 1936 near Lake Victoria in Alego, Kenya, and was lucky to be studying in the United States. Although he was, by all accounts, a remarkable student, he was also mischievous and had gotten kicked out of the prestigious Maseno School in Kenya for troublemaking and skipping class. His father, Hussein Onyango Obama, was disappointed in him, fearing that he wouldn't succeed in life because he wasn't taking his education seriously. His mother, Akumu, Onyango's second wife, had left the family when Barack Sr. and his sister, Sarah, were small because she thought that Onyango was too strict. So Barack and Sarah were raised by Sarah Hussein Onyango, their stepmother and Onyango's third wife. (In many nations in Africa, men are allowed by custom and law to have several wives at one time.)

Barack grew close to his stepmother, but his sister, Sarah, remained loyal to their mother, Akumu, and resented her father because he didn't think girls needed an education. Onyango had taken pride in Barack's intelligence as a youth and wanted his son to be as educated as the white people he knew. Barack found school boring and would not go for weeks, yet when it came time for exams, he would study the lessons himself, take the tests, and come in first! When Barack was expelled, Onyango sent him to Mombasa on the coast of Kenya to work as a clerk.

Barack couldn't keep a job for long because he often spoke up when his bosses were making decisions that he thought were not good ones, angering his employers. He was stubborn with a sharp wit, strong opinions, and a strong moral character, which meant that he didn't let things go when he thought people were behaving badly or unjustly. When Barack was no longer welcome at a job, he would find other low-skill, low-paying work, but it wouldn't challenge him. And he stopped practicing Islam, the religion of his father, or any religion for that matter.

Soon he got distracted by talk of Kenya's fight for independence from "white rule" (the United Kingdom). Kenyans wanted to run their own country, the way Americans had wanted freedom from the British during the American Revolutionary War almost two hundred years earlier. The Kenyans wanted to be treated equally to white people and eventually won their independence in 1963. At the same time blacks and progressive white people were fighting for equal rights for all Americans during the Civil Rights Movement in the United States.

While working various clerking jobs, Barack met a woman named Kezia and married her. His father initially refused to give them his blessing in the form of a dowry (a gift to the parents of the bride). But soon Onyango gave in, and Barack and Kezia welcomed a child into their family: a boy named Roy.

Barack's friends who had stayed in school were now attending universities in Uganda, another African country, and England, a country in Europe. Barack realized that he had to start behaving like a grown-up and make something of his life, especially since he had a family to support. One day he met two American women teachers who told him he still had a chance to pursue higher education if he took a correspondence course. He worked on his lessons at home and mailed in his homework for grading. After a few months he knew enough to take the final exam, and months after that, he received word that he'd passed! Now he could go to university! However, Barack didn't have any money to pay for school, so he wrote to several universities in the United

States explaining his situation. After a long time, the University of Hawaii replied—the only place to do so—and offered him full tuition. They would pay for his education.

Barack asked his stepmother, Sarah, if, while he was away, she would take care of his son, Roy, and his wife, Kezia, who was pregnant again, this time with a girl she'd later name Auma. In no time Barack, at twenty-three years old, set out for Hawaii, the newest state in America's union.

When eighteen-year-old Stanley Ann Dunham, better known as Ann, met Barack Obama, Sr., in their Russian language class at the university, she thought he was handsome, principled, and brilliant. He was the first, and only, African student studying there then. She told her parents about the boy she'd gotten to know from Kenya, and they insisted that she invite him over. At dinner, they too were impressed by his manners and swift mind.

For their first date, Ann and Barack were to meet at the library at one o'clock in the afternoon. She arrived on time, but Barack was late, so Ann decided to give him a few minutes to show up while she got some sun reclining on a bench. Without intending to, she fell asleep and an hour later, Barack arrived with three friends. Barack, who had a habit of bragging to others, declared that Ann was a good woman because she had waited for him. In Kenya, women were expected to obey the men they married.

Although Ann was willing to compromise at times, and

put other people's wishes before hers, she was an independent thinker. She had spent her childhood doing things her own way, in spite of what other kids thought of her. She was not afraid to stand alone. Her father, Stanley Armour Dunham, who was raised Baptist, and her mother, Madelyn Lee Payne, whom he'd met when they both lived in Wichita, Kansas, were also liberal-minded.

Before Ann was born, Stanley had promised Madelyn that they would be free spirits and live a life of adventure. They eloped in 1940. A year and a half later, the United States got involved in World War II when the Japanese bombed Pearl Harbor in Hawaii on December 7, 1941. On January 18, Stanley enlisted in the army at Fort Leavenworth, Kansas. Madelyn gave birth to Stanley Ann Dunham (named after her father because he had wanted a boy) on an army base on November 29, 1942, and later, when Stanley returned from his tour of duty, they all moved to California. Stanley tried taking courses at a local college, but his desire for adventure got the best of him. They moved back to Kansas and then to Texas, where they encountered their first real taste of the racism that seemed to drench the United States at that time.

At the furniture store where he worked, Stanley was warned not to help black or Mexican customers until the shop was closed. That way the white customers would not have to be in the store at the same time as black or Mexican people. Madelyn, who worked at a bank, was scolded for politely referring to a black janitor as "mister," as in "Mr. Reed."

This was a man, a patriot, who had served in World War II, just as Madelyn's husband had, and yet, because of his skin color, he was treated differently—disrespectfully. Stanley and Madelyn were sickened by this inequality, and though they tried to hide their feelings from Ann, who was not yet a teenager at the time, their daughter was sharp enough to catch on.

One day Madelyn returned from work at the bank and came upon a group of children clustered outside the picket fence bordering her home. They were shouting vulgar things, including the n-word. Madelyn saw that her daughter was lying beside a tree with a playmate, a black girl her age. A child outside the fence threw a stone at the girls, and Madelyn noticed that the two girls were terrified and upset. She suggested that they go with her inside the house, but the black child ran away as soon as Madelyn reached for her. When Stanley learned what had happened, he confronted the neighbors about the behavior of their children. He was told that he needed to have a talk with his own child, because in that town, children of different races didn't play together. Not too long afterward, the family moved to Seattle, Washington, in part to escape the injustice around them. Ann would soon attend Mercer Island High School, and Stanley briefly enrolled the family in a Unitarian Universalist congregation because he liked how that religion was inclusive and embraced teachings of several different faiths.

Ann was an exceptional student. At sixteen, she was accepted to the University of Chicago, but her father thought she was too young to live on her own and wouldn't let her go. The entire family eventually moved to Honolulu, Hawaii, where a furniture store owned by the same company for which Stanley worked in Seattle was opening up. Ann enrolled in the university there to study anthropology.

Soon, in 1960, Barack Obama, Sr., and Ann Dunham were in love and planned to marry. Barack, who was studying econometrics (essentially using math to figure out how to help a nation control and distribute its wealth), wrote home to his father in Kenya about the engagement. Onyango was not happy about the union because he believed that white people's customs and priorities were different from Africans'. He didn't think that Ann would return to Kenya with Barack to live as a Luo woman. He knew that white people did not believe a man should have more than one wife, and Barack had another wife at home. (Ann had gotten the sense that Barack and his wife from Kenya were separated and no longer bound to each other.) Onyango felt that Ann's father should visit him in Kenya so they could talk in person about the marriage, since, according to Kenyan custom, marriages were to be arranged by the parents. But most important, Onyango believed that returning to Kenya was Barack's duty, as the people of Kenya looked to Barack as someone who would help fix their troubled government. A man with such smarts and an education from the United States had to invest his time and energy in helping his family—and, in spirit, everyone in Kenya was family.

Ann's parents loved Barack. They enjoyed it when he gave them his assessment of politics or government. Stanley even began taking an interest in those things and the political discourse and racial dynamics of America. But they were also worried that their daughter wanted to marry Barack— a black man from Africa. Perhaps they were afraid of how Ann would be treated in America, since it was against the law in most of the United States for a white person to marry a "Negro," a person of African descent. Not only was it against the law, but if somebody got it in his head to capture Barack and hang him by his neck until he was dead, law enforcement, especially in some southern states, most likely would have looked the other way, because black people were not given the same protections as people of other races.

Hawaii was somewhat different from the rest of the states. It had just joined the union and wasn't as caught up in the same racial divides that haunted the rest of the nation. The group of islands was home to a diverse population of people, though it too had its own troubled history. Ann and Barack believed that they could make their marriage work in Hawaii or any other place. So they wed in a civil ceremony, with very few others in attendance.

Barack excelled in his studies at the university. He started the International Students Association and became its first president. In 1961, on August 4, Ann gave birth to their son, Barack Hussein Obama, Jr. (whom they called "Barry" or "Bar" for short).

Barack Hussein Obama, Jr., was born at the Kapi'olani Medical Center for Women and Children in Honolulu, Hawaii. The name Barack means "blessed" in Swahili and Arabic, and Hussein means "beautiful."

Barack Sr. was intent on furthering his education with a PhD degree. After finishing a four-year program in three years, he received word in 1963 that he had been awarded a full scholarship to the New School in New York City. He had also been given a full scholarship to Harvard University. However, the Harvard scholarship would not cover the cost of bringing his family with him, while the award from the New School would, by providing him with housing and a job on campus. For Barack Sr., there was only one option. He felt he needed to go to Harvard in order to get the best education possible, because Harvard was known worldwide as an exceptional school. That meant the people of Kenya would have heard of the school and would recognize that Barack had done as well as any person could. Barack Sr. had already left one wife behind in Kenya. He'd seen it as a necessary sacrifice. He made the same decision again.

While Barack Sr. was away at school, Ann had time to think about her future with him. Her mother, Madelyn, had heard about the Mau Mau rebellion in Kenya and knew there was a fight for independence going on. She was afraid

Barack Obama, Jr., with his mother, Ann, and riding a tricycle, in Hawaii in the early 1960s. Tourists were sometimes curious about his background and assumed he was Hawaiian.

for her daughter's life and didn't want her moving there. By the time Barack Sr. had completed his PhD degree, Ann had decided she no longer wanted to be in their marriage. So Barack Sr. returned to Kenya without his American wife and son. And Barack Jr., like his father before him, would grow up missing one of his parents.

"... If fate causes us
to stumble and fall,
our larger American family
will be there to lift us up."[3]

CHAPTER
TWO

Madelyn felt she was too young to be called "Granny." On the day Barack Jr. was born, she insisted her family call her "tutu," the Hawaiian word for "grandparent," which the clan later shortened to "Toot." Barack learned about his father from the stories she, her husband, Stanley ("Gramps"), and his mother would tell him. They were wonderful stories, mythic in scale, poetic in their significance. Barack's dad came across as a legend and a hero, accomplishing great things in some noble fight for justice.

Gramps told the story, with Toot and Ann chiming in, of how the elder Barack had taken a friend, another African student, for a sightseeing trip and was swerving all over the road in the car because he was used to driving on the other side of the street in Kenya. At the top of the hill, his friend asked to try Barack Sr.'s pipe. Barack Sr. eventually let him, but his friend accidentally dropped the pipe over the cliff railing. Barack Sr.'s father, Onyango, had taught his son to respect other people's things, and Barack Sr. thought that his friend had not shown the proper respect for his property. So he lifted his friend in the air and made believe that he was going to drop him too. Everyone was in a panic. Though Barack Sr. finally put his friend down, Ann was upset that he had behaved rashly and scared them all. But the way Gramps told the story, the incident was more of a practical joke. Gramps found the whole thing hilarious.

There were many tales the trio recounted to the younger Barack that filled his mind with grand images of his father. Ann recalled the time when Barry's dad, while at the University of Hawaii, arrived to accept a great honor: his key from the Phi Beta Kappa society, in recognition of academic excellence. He was dressed in his favorite blue jeans, while the rest of the crowd was decked out in tuxedos. It was the one time in his life that Ann saw him embarrassed. But there were few indignities that could break his spirit.

His family sometimes discussed the time Barry's father had taken a break from studying to relax with Gramps and some friends at a bar. There was a man there who had issues with black people, and said out loud that he shouldn't have to sit next to one, and he used a derogatory term. Instead of losing his cool, which most people expected him to do, Barack Sr. went up to the man, smiled, and gave him one long lecture on human rights, dignity, and the absurdity of racism. By the time Barack Sr. had finished educating him, the man felt so ashamed of himself he gave Barack $100 as penance. Few but those who were there could believe it.

Even without him in his life, Barry felt his father's presence through photo albums and countless anecdotes. Meanwhile, Gramps had become Barry's surrogate father. He took the child spearfishing with one of his clients off Kailua Bay. In one of Barack's earliest childhood memories, he recalls sitting up high on his grandfather's shoulders watching the astronauts return to Hickam Air Force Base after splashing down in the ocean. If you listened to Gramps tell it, though, he'd swear that an astronaut had waved at Barack and Barack alone, and that Barack had waved back. Gramps wanted Barack to know that he was special—and well loved.

Barack's mixed-race heritage was met with both curiosity and ignorance outside his family. Gramps noticed that tourists often behaved insensitively or made uninformed remarks about Barry. To those who mistook Barack for Hawaiian when he was having fun at the beach, Gramps gave a resounding tongue-lashing on Barack's true background. To those who stared at Barack playing in the sand, unsure what to make of him or how to categorize him, Gramps offered a story for the ages: He claimed Barack was the great-grandson of King Kamehameha. Gramps reveled in their reactions as they snapped photo after photo of Barack, thinking they were in the presence of royalty.

Barack's family did their best to shield him from the complications of race in America, complications of identity that most white people don't have to confront. They regaled him with memories of his father that were inspiring in order to prove to Barack that he had come from greatness. The wondrous details in their accounts kept Barack from questioning too much and asking the toughest question of all: If his father was so great, then why wasn't he around?

"We may come from
        different places
and have **different stories,**
        but **we share common**
hopes, and one very
                American dream."[4]

"Government alone can't teach our kids to learn."[5]

When Barack was four, another man

entered his life: Lolo Soetoro. Lolo, which means "crazy" in
Hawaiian (and which Gramps thought was hysterical), was
from Indonesia. He had met Barack's mother at the university. They dated for two years and then decided to get married. Lolo suddenly had to return to Indonesia, so Ann
remained in the United States and spent months preparing
for her and Barack's journey to join Lolo there, which included collecting the proper documentation, such as passports
and visas, to enter and live in a different country. Ever the

protective parent, Toot called the State Department to make sure Indonesia was a stable country where her child and grandchild would be safe. Part of Ann's desire to leave Hawaii was to get out from under the watchful eyes of her parents and do something big, something great for another country in need. Gramps, in the meantime, got six-year-old Barack interested in the geography of the Indonesian islands.

Their journey to Jakarta took several days and included a stopover in Japan. Once they arrived in Indonesia, Lolo met them at the airport and drove them home, passing an enormous statue of Hanuman, the monkey god from the Hindu culture. (Lolo practiced a form of Islam that incorporated ideas from other belief systems.) When they arrived at their stucco-and-red-tile house at 16 Haji Ramli Street, they were greeted by a big surprise: A wild gibbon named Tata, an ape that Barack mistook for a monkey, leaped from branch to branch in the tree above their heads. Lolo had brought Tata from New Guinea, an island north of Australia, all the way to Indonesia, just for Barack. There were also alligators, ducks, and chickens living in their yard.

The family could not afford for Barack to attend the International School where most of the children of foreigners studied. Instead he went to two primary schools in Jakarta: Sekolah Dasar Negeri 04 Besuki (SDN 04), and the Catholic school Franciscus Assisi. In first grade he wrote an essay titled "I Want to Become President" for his teacher Israella Pareira Darmawan. And then again in the third grade his teacher, Fermina Katarina Sinaga, said Barry (as he was known then) included in his "My Dream: What I Want to Be in the Future" assignment that he wanted to be "a President." He had set big goals for himself early on. His schoolmates, who knew him as Barry Soetoro, sometimes called him "Curly Eyelashes" because his lashes were so long and curly.

Ann had made efforts to teach Barack additional lessons through an American correspondence course, similar to what his dad had done years before. As for herself, she found work at the American Embassy teaching English to Indonesian businessmen. Lolo worked as a geologist for the army.

Now Barry had Lolo to look up to, to help him learn the ways of the world. Part of that lesson included figuring out how to protect himself from other children looking for a fight. Lolo bought Barack boxing gloves and showed him how to move around so he could avoid getting hit when swung at. In this way Barack got to spend time alone with Lolo, participating in activities fathers often share with their sons. Barack mastered Lolo's language and customs in less than a year. Lolo taught him how to eat small, green, hot-chili peppers raw, and introduced him to other local cuisine staples (such as snake, grasshopper, and dog!). When talking to other people, Lolo referred to Barack as his son. Barack enjoyed the adventure into which Lolo had brought him and his mother.

There were some things, though, about life in Indonesia that left Barry feeling confused. He didn't know what the disease leprosy was until it stared him in the face in the form of a man whose nose was missing. There were droughts, which meant that it didn't rain enough during growing season for crops to grow, and then there were floods, when it rained so much people's houses and livestock got swept away. Barry's mother seemed as confused by these things, grasping for answers she didn't have when he needed them. So Barry sought out Lolo, who tended to have less of an emotional response to these events.

Lolo considered himself more practical than Barack's mom. Though she felt compelled to give money to the countless beggars they'd encounter, Lolo thought that attempting to help people in this small way was unwise. He challenged Barack to consider how little money he had, and compare that to how many beggars there were on the street. If he kept giving his money away, Lolo suggested, Barack would be left with nothing too. When Barack asked Lolo about the leech scars on his leg, which Lolo had gotten while wading through the swamps of New Guinea, Lolo let Barack know that having leeches on his skin had hurt, but that sometimes one must look past the pain toward where one wants to end up.

Moving to Indonesia had been difficult for Barack's mother, Ann, not because it was a place she had never been before, with customs she had never experienced and a chaotic past she knew of only from books, but because she

Barack attended elementary school in Jakarta, Indonesia; here he's shown with classmates, around fourth grade.

Barack's mother and Lolo had a daughter named Maya. Her full name is Maya Soetoro-Ng, and she is Barack's half sister. This photo was taken in Honolulu in 2007.

and Lolo were not communicating the way they had back in Hawaii. Lolo seemed to have changed. He didn't speak much to Ann anymore or acknowledge her worries. In fact, few words ever seemed to pass between them.

Ann felt very alone. She thought Lolo had become more interested in practical ideas like getting by and getting ahead than in less concrete and, some might argue, larger ideals such as moral integrity. Lolo seemed willing to compromise his beliefs for the sake of securing a better life for his family. He hid their refrigerator, which cost two month's salary, when tax officials came to see how much the family owed the government. He did this because the officials would see the fridge as a sign that they owned more things and therefore owed more tax money. Lolo didn't see the differences between right and wrong in black-and-white terms. He eventually worked his way up into the government relations office of an American oil company. Most people would see this as success. Ann didn't see it that way.

Lolo hadn't always been so hardened. But the political climate in Indonesia in the late 1960s had made everyone afraid. He hadn't wanted to return to Indonesia from Hawaii so quickly. But the government had forced all students studying abroad to come back and stripped them of their passports. Because the people in government had taken control of individuals' lives, Lolo was immediately drafted into the army and sent to New Guinea. Those who tried to resist and fight the government didn't survive. In the face of that kind of fear—fear for one's life and livelihood—it is difficult to stand up to people in power. Some people think, "If you can't beat 'em, join 'em." That was not the lesson Ann wanted Barack to learn.

Honesty. Principles. These were the characteristics of a man whom Ann had loved dearly: The absent father of her young son. Barack's present father figure didn't exactly share those same values. On which side of these influences was her child going to fall?

Even in those dangerous times, Ann was determined not to let her child accept corruption. She started waking him up every school day at four in the morning for his English lessons and she wouldn't let him out of them, no matter what sort of excuses he gave. She taught Barack about the Civil Rights struggle in America and gave him the speeches of Dr. Martin Luther King, Jr., to study and recordings of Mahalia Jackson to listen to. The plight of black people in America was at least as bad as that of any other group, and Ann chose to educate her son on the choices and advances the most courageous among them were making. Ann insisted that Barack remember he got more than his name from his dad. He also inherited his father's character and his ethics. Yet for Barack, that man was little more than an illusion: a collection of short stories. It was getting harder to follow in the footsteps of a ghost.

Barry and his mother went to the embassy so she could finish up some work. Barry did his homework in the library and then tried to find other things to read to entertain himself. He still remembers leafing through a magazine, looking at the different photos, trying to guess what was happening in each news story. One image struck him as unusual. A man with white skin had features that were more like his own, more like his dad's. He read on and realized that this man had bleached himself with a chemical the advertisers promised would turn him into a white person. That was supposed to make him happy—skinning himself alive! Apparently thousands of black people had tried it. Although the man expressed regret about it, Barack started to wonder why someone would do something so extreme in order to change the color of his skin in the first place.

Through the next year, with the birth of his half sister, Maya, and the completion of his American correspondence course, Barack, at nine years old, started to see the world through different eyes. He started to see that the color of his skin—a shade of his father—was something many people were desperate to escape. He wondered if he should be running from it too.

"The library has always been . . . a place where we've come to discover big ideas and profound concepts that help move the American story forward."[6]

"**Don't think** that fatherhood **ends** at conception. I know something about that because **my father wasn't around** when I was young and **I struggled.**"[7]

CHAPTER
FOUR

In the time that Barack had been away,

Gramps and Toot had moved into a two-bedroom apartment on Beretania Street in Honolulu. Toot had done well at the local bank and been promoted to vice president—the first woman to reach that level. Gramps, meanwhile, had left the furniture business and now sold life insurance. But since he didn't really believe people needed what he was selling, his heart wasn't in it, and he had a hard time making an income.

Barry, at ten years old, returned to Hawaii by himself

to live with his grandparents. His mother wanted him to study in America since he had finished all the lessons in his correspondence course, and because Gramps, with help from his boss, an alumnus of the Punahou Academy prep school, had gotten Barry admitted to that same prestigious school. Ann reassured Barack with the promise that she and Maya would return within a year's time and also be home for Christmas. Plus, he wouldn't have to wake up at four in the morning any longer to study.

In the fall, Gramps accompanied Barack to his first day of school at Punahou. Barack introduced himself as "Barry" to a boy named Ronald, then Gramps walked the two of them to room 307 in Castle Hall, Miss Hefty's class. Inside, Miss Hefty used Barack's given name, which surprised Ronald. Many of the children laughed at the sound of it. Miss Hefty ignored the snickers and went on to explain that she had been a teacher in Kenya, and Gramps had told her Barack's dad was from there. Which tribe did Barack's father come from? she wondered.

Barack could barely believe what he had been asked in front of a room full of students he didn't know. He told her his father was from the Luo tribe, and a child hooted the word, imitating a monkey.

Later that day a boy asked Barack if his father ate people, perpetuating a lie that people from African countries were cannibals. Another day a girl with red hair asked if she could touch Barack's hair, as though he were a novelty or specimen—an organism under a microscope to be studied.

Barack wouldn't let her touch him and backed away as she reached for his curly afro.

Barack didn't feel as though he fit in with his classmates. Most had grown up together and had attended the same schools since they were very young. None of them wore the sandals he'd grown accustomed to in Jakarta. They didn't know how to play soccer or chess or badminton, and he couldn't throw a football properly or ride a skateboard.

There was only one other black child in Barack's grade: a girl. Perhaps because people expected them to gravitate toward each other due to the sameness of their skin color, she and he avoided one another as though they were like-poled magnets. One day, purely out of chance, they ended up playing together—just the two of them—on the playground. But in the middle of their fun, a group of children started teasing them, saying Barack had a girlfriend. Maybe subconsciously the other children thought that because they were the only black children there, Barack and this little girl were destined to end up together—they couldn't see them with anyone else. Barack felt attacked and shoved the girl, perhaps because that's what boys do when teased about girls, but more likely because he wanted to prove to himself and all the others that skin color—his skin color—didn't matter. He didn't want it. So he pushed the color away.

Children teased Barack less after that and he felt he did a better job of blending in, but at what cost to his self-worth? Then one day Toot told him about the telegram she had received. His father was coming to visit at Christmastime, the same time as his mother and Maya.

Barack's dad had remarried and was the father of five sons and one daughter in Kenya. He was coming to visit as part of his recovery after surviving a terrible car accident. Barack's mom wanted very badly for her son and his father to get along—for the reunion to go smoothly. She got a book on Kenya written by the first president of the nation, Jomo Kenyatta. His name meant "burning spear." She flooded Barack with facts about the nation, including snippets on the Luo people.

The day of his dad's arrival, Miss Hefty let Barack out of school early. At home he hesitated and stalled outside of Toot's door, not wanting to go in. When finally he entered, he saw his dad: tall, the color of midnight, hobbled by his leg injury. He was skinnier than Barack thought he'd be, in no way Herculean enough to hoist a man above his head. The whites of his eyes behind his glasses were yellow, as though an egg yolk had blended with its albumen. Could this man be the titan Barack had heard about his whole life?

His father, before retiring to take a nap that afternoon, handed Barack three wooden figurines from his bag—carvings handmade in Kenya of a man and two wild animals, a lion and an elephant.

Barack felt let down by his father's realness. So he chose instead to force-feed his friends the image of his dad that he'd once held on to—that of a great, important leader. He told them Olympian-sized tales about him, even bigger than

Punahou Academy is a private school located in Honolulu, Hawaii. Barack enrolled in 1971, when he was ten; students still attend the school today.

This photo of Barack and his father was taken when Barack Obama, Sr., came to visit Barack and Ann in Hawaii in 1971.

the ones he had grown up with, fables he knew weren't true. He told some boys his dad was a prince, that men were fighting to take his dad's place as chief of the tribe, but that one day, if he wanted to, Barack could become a prince too. He told them Obama meant "burning spear," for the men in his family were great warriors. He wanted it all to be true. He wanted to believe the myth.

Barry's family started growing comfortable with Barack Sr.'s presence. His dad seemed to win them all over—he had a charm that put them at ease and an intelligence that excited them, for a spell. Then they started to grow weary of their guest. He seemed to expect to be treated like the head of a family of which he was no longer part.

How the Grinch Stole Christmas was on television, and Barack sat down to watch it. It was only shown once a year, and Barack had been waiting all week for it to air. His father, however, insisted that Barack turn off the television and study. And if he was already done with his schoolwork, he should read up on the next day's or week's lessons.

Gramps, Toot, Barack Sr., and Ann all argued about which of them controlled the household and Barack Jr. Everyone laid claims to being his guardian. He was living with his grandparents, who were taking care of him; his mother, though she lived in Indonesia, was still his mom; and his father, whom he hadn't seen for eight years, was still his dad. Barack didn't like how testy people had become around his father. He realized then that he was ready for his dad to leave.

The next day, however, his mother told him that Miss Hefty had invited Barry's dad to speak to his class. Barry knew he was caught. How was he going to explain that all the stories he'd told, the pictures he'd painted, the mythology he had built around his father were lies? How would his classmates react to that reality? How could Barack himself face the truth?

But his father was a hit. The children ate up his stories about how mankind was born from the earth in Africa. He described wild animals—lions, elephants—in their natural world. He talked about Luo traditions and the practices of the tribe. And he talked about Kenya's fights for independence and freedom for the enslaved, similar to battles that had been fought in America.

Barack Sr. had lived up to his titanic reputation. Even the boy who had shamed Barack with jokes about his father eating people was tamed and impressed. With that speech, Barack's connection to his father was forged. He wanted to spend as much time as he could with his dad and imitate him, and learn what he knew. Barack now recognized how it felt to want his father home.

The day before he left, Barack's dad found some music he had brought with him for Barack. The sounds were from his native Kenya: guitars, drums, and a joyous chorus of voices. His father started dancing and waited for Barack to join him. Barack took his first steps, a young boy before his father.

"... Ensuring that **every American child** gets the **best education** possible is the new civil rights challenge of our time."[8]

CHAPTER
FIVE

Barack lived with his mother and younger

half sister, Maya, in Hawaii. His mother and Lolo had separated. He'd stayed in Indonesia and she'd returned to the University of Hawaii to get a master's degree in anthropology not long after Barry's father's return to Kenya. Ann was a single parent with two children residing in a small apartment a block away from Barry's school, living off her student grants and, on occasion, food stamps.

Barry was among the poorer students at Punahou Academy, though few other students knew it. The school was made up of mostly white children from wealthier families, along with Asians and Hawaiians. If Barry was teased at all these days, it was for having the initials B.O., or for being slightly chubby and somewhat different—not quite Hawaiian or Samoan, definitely not white.

His mother had to complete her fieldwork and decided to return to Indonesia to do so. Barry had no interest in going back and being new and different all over again. He and his grandparents had an understanding that he could live with them whenever. Besides, he was now searching for ways to become a black man like his dad, but he had no clue how. What he had left of his father were memories from their brief encounter and the occasional letter with a Kenyan postmark, more like souvenirs from a trip he'd taken, pieces of the past, than anything he could relate to day to day.

Ann left for Asia once again with Maya, and Barack leaned on Gramps and Gramps's black male friends for guidance. Gramps would take Barack out at night to different nightclubs to play pool or to someone's home to play poker. One of Gramps's friends was Frank Marshall Davis, a man well into his eighties who had lived through many of America's internal struggles and formed opinions about the state of blacks in society, based on his own experiences. He wrote poetry and made friends with people who did not believe in democracy, because he thought black people had a better chance of achieving equality under a different type of government. As it turned out, neither system of government lived up to the promise of equality for all. Barack looked to Frank for some hint of whom he should become as an adult. But he also looked to television, music, and movies for examples. Pop culture, too, would become his role model.

Then there was basketball. His father had given Barack a basketball for Christmas, and Gramps had taken Barack to see the University of Hawaii team play in the spring. All five of the starting players were black . . . and stars in Barack's eyes. The very idea of the sport transformed him. Barack practiced for hours after school each day until dark on a nearby playground. Eventually he started getting into pickup games with older African-American men who played on the Chamberlain Field courts at the university. They taught him the attitude and swagger that helped turn his game from one of just physical prowess into one that included mental gamesmanship. He replaced intermediate football in eighth grade with basketball and part-time work at a neighborhood Baskin-Robbins with junior varsity basketball in tenth.

Barry had started making friends with other black boys who had found themselves in Hawaii at Punahou Academy. One of them, Keith, became a close friend of his. Keith struggled with identity issues as a black male too, but his opinion of his environment and situation differed from Barack's. Keith seemed to have an unspoken understanding of the reasons why he might be slighted by white people or be called derogatory names. He saw it as a flaw of the entire white race, not individuals. So Barack practiced his rage with Keith and turned his anger outward. He used his fists the way Lolo had taught him to in response to kids who aimed words at him that caused him pain. He got angry at white people in general for injustices, real or imagined, for which he thought each and every one of them was responsible. Barack, however, had a parent and grandparents who had never been anything but loving and supportive. Was his family the exception to the rule, or were the rules something neither he nor Keith completely understood?

In high school, Barack started reading the works of famous black men to help him learn more about where society expected him to end up. He read books like *Invisible Man*, by Ralph Ellison, and *Native Son*, by Richard Wright. He read W.E.B. DuBois and Langston Hughes, a contemporary of his older friend Frank Davis. What he realized, however, was that each of these men hadn't found a solution to American racism. Each had died disenchanted and resigned to the idea that the fate of black people in America was sealed in a coffin of oppression.

Only the final works of Malcolm X showed some promise of hope. Barry's mother didn't understand his interest in following a movement that sought to exclude everyone but black people from it. But only "X," at the end of his short life, seemed to think a reconciliation between black and white was possible. Barack needed to believe that racial harmony could be attained, as he had been born a shade of gray, so to speak. How could he find inner peace if there was no hope for outward unity?

On the basketball court, race didn't seem to matter; or perhaps it did, but that small 84-by-50-foot plane was the only place in the world where Barack and his black friends felt they finally had an advantage. Barack ultimately went all the way to the varsity level as the left-handed backup forward, helping the team take the state championship against Moanalua High School, 60–28, in 1979, his senior year. Off the courts, he and his black friends found other diversions. Parties, movies, talking smack—or running their mouths. And disco. The 1970s was a great time for music and for learning new dance moves. Not coincidentally, the musicians they idolized, like Stevie Wonder, Miles Davis, and Marvin Gaye, were largely black. Few of the Hawaiian and Asian students paid attention to that fact—they only thought of them, their cultural heroes, as "nonwhite" like most of the Hawaiian population. But Barack took notice.

One evening, Toot and Gramps had an argument. Toot had been frightened by a beggar asking for money who wouldn't leave her alone. Barry didn't understand what the fighting was all about, until Gramps told him that the beggar was black and that's why Toot had been so scared. Barack was stunned both by the idea that his grandfather could suspect his grandmother of racism, and by the idea that his grandmother could maybe, just maybe, harbor a deep-seated fear of black people.

Barack went to see Gramps's friend Frank Davis. Frank explained what he thought was going on: Even though Barack's grandparents had open hearts and generous spirits, they

WE GO PLAY HOOP

Thanks Tut, Gramps, Choom Gang, and Ray for all the good times.

Barry Obama

"Barry" enjoyed basketball in high school at Punahou. The photo on the right is Barack's senior yearbook picture.

Toot and Gramps, shown here with Barack at his high school graduation.

came from a different world, with different upbringings, where black people lived in the background if they were there at all. There was no need to try to understand black people, since people like his grandparents had little interaction with them. It would be near impossible for them or any white people to get what it's like to be nonwhite anyway, no matter how much they wanted to, no matter how many black friends (or servants) they had. For blacks, understanding white people was a matter of survival; for whites, getting to know blacks was more of a diversion.

Barack took this to heart and turned inward. He started giving up on his future and all the things his mother had told him he needed to succeed, like education, goals, and principles. His friend Keith went away to community college, and Barack allowed his grades to slip. He had stopped writing to his father, and the letters from Kenya ceased coming in return. He continued using basketball as an escape, but he also started smoking cigarettes and using illegal drugs to numb his anger and hide his hopelessness. He started down a path leading nowhere fast. He was fulfilling the destiny he thought white people expected him to fulfill: that of failure. He sat back as friends of his fell to powerlessness: killed in car crashes, busted by police for having or using drugs. That's where he was headed. He didn't seem to care.

His mother, having finished her fieldwork, was again in Hawaii and confronted him one day about his lackadaisical attitude regarding his education. Barry told her he was thinking of not going away to college and maybe just going to the university part-time. After all she had struggled to do and the example she had tried to set for her son, here he was without an ounce of ambition. This certainly was not his father's son. Or hers. She didn't understand what had happened to his drive. Barack questioned her reaction since Gramps hadn't even gone to college. Was she worried he'd end up like Gramps?

Gramps still struggled with work, which was a point of tension between him and Toot. Was Ann ashamed that she and her mother had done more in their lives than her father? Gramps was the man who had had such big dreams for his wife and daughter yet never went to college himself and kept Ann from going early, perhaps to keep her close to home. Ann had done a lot in her young adulthood to break free from his control; she may have wondered why her son would choose to follow the path her father had paved.

Ann answered Barack curtly and left the room. Their interaction bothered Barack a lot. He continued to go through the motions at school so as not to upset her anymore, graduating from high school and planning to attend Occidental College in Los Angeles (mainly because a girl he liked lived in that city).

Before Barack left for college, he stopped by to see Frank one last time. Frank, however, saw college as a compromise— black people giving up the fight, agreeing to live by rules and restrictions imposed upon them by white society. Frank thought black people in college got trained to obey like dogs.

Barack wondered what Frank would have him do instead. Frank replied that Barack still needed to go to college, but he needed to go with his eyes open, aware of what could happen to him if he got too comfortable there. Frank told Barack to "stay awake."

"I was not born into money or status. I was born to a teenage mom in Hawaii, and my dad left us when I was two. But my family gave me love, they gave me education, and most of all, they gave me hope— hope that in America, no dream is beyond our grasp if we reach for it, and fight for it, and work for it."[9]

Barry Obama entered Occidental College

with a full scholarship in 1979. He found the student body there to be fairly diverse, and he decided he needed to choose a crowd in which to belong. The decision for him was easy. He had already aligned himself with the black students at Punahou, and Frank had told him that in order to stay black, he needed to stay awake. So Barry associated with the black students who kept to themselves—the ones who thought the only way to survive was to stay close to one another. Their discussions seemed like an extension of the ones he'd begun all those years ago with his friend Keith and Gramps's friend Frank. Yet as much as Barry contributed to their talks about the struggles of black people, he wasn't even sure he belonged in that group.

There was one woman who refused to choose sides. She, like Barry, was of mixed heritage, but her approach to race was different. In fact, she tended to avoid black people because she felt pressure from them to align herself with black people—a pressure she didn't get from whites. However, Barry realized, this was what Frank was talking about: losing yourself and your culture by adopting someone else's customs—blending in with the people who hold the power. And yet, even if one does everything one can to blend in, one cannot change one's skin color. She and Barry could never be fully accepted as white. Someone—from either side of the aisle—would have something to say about it.

Barry's favorite teacher was Roger Boesche, who taught a class on modern political thought. Mr. Boesche helped Barry think more about the world around him and less about himself. He even gave Barry a B on a paper, when he clearly deserved an A, just to challenge him. Through his actions, Mr. Boesche dared Barack to push himself academically in order to reach his potential.

Barry sought out the people who lived on the fringe of society or had forward-thinking ideas: the punk rockers, the black activists, the radicals, the Hispanics, the feminist crowd. These were people with whom he thought he could discuss ideas about human rights and the problems in government. Everyone else, he thought, was part of the problem, not the solution. But even among these groups, Barry felt like a fake. It was as though he needed to go to extremes to prove his loyalty to their causes. Once, he talked behind someone's back, saying the boy wasn't "black enough," meaning he wasn't well connected with his culture because he chose to use correct grammar when he spoke or he didn't feel drawn to discussing black issues. But that backfired with his friend, a leader whose sister was a founding member of a Midwest chapter of the Black Panther Party. (The Black Panthers were a nationalist party whose goal was to uplift the black community and protect it from social injustices, such as police brutality and other threats to civil rights.) Barry was trying so hard to prove to the leaders of these crowds that he was one of them that he didn't realize the person he was really trying to convince was himself.

One day, Barry had a conversation with a young black woman at the library and they spoke about their respective upbringings. She asked him why people called him Barry and not Barack. He told her that his father had been called Barry when he came to the United States, perhaps because it was easier to pronounce and helped him fit in. The name just got transferred to Barry by default. She decided that she liked the name Barack, and its meaning, better. Barry told her she could call him Barack, as long as she said it right. She then went on about her childhood in Chicago. She had an absent father, just like Barack. She lived in a rough place where there was never enough heat in the apartment in the winter and no air-conditioning in the summer, leaving people to sleep outside by the lake at night to stay cool. But her life was filled with extended family. Uncles, cousins, and grandparents all gathered together in the kitchen, laughing. It seemed like a magical fantasy life to Barack and he told her so. She then admitted she'd been wishing she'd grown up in Hawaii.

Barack and his politically active friends took on a new cause in 1980, his sophomore year in college. White people, mainly from Holland and Britain, had moved to a country filled with Africans many years before and decided that they should run it. Apartheid was a policy in South Africa in which it was mandatory that the white, Indian, and black races remain separate, similar to the Jim Crow laws in the United States that started in the 1880s and lasted through most of the 1960s. Not only that, the few white people who lived in South Africa made most of the money by excluding black people from having good jobs, forcing them into servitude and poverty. This is also what it was like in the American south for black people when Barack's mother was growing up.

Some Americans had decided that apartheid was unfair, and they held demonstrations, often on college campuses, in efforts to draw international attention to that injustice. They wanted to pressure their government to force the South Africans to get rid of apartheid. If the United States refused to trade with South Africa and boycotted businesses that dealt with it, South Africa would lose a lot of money and have to alter its policies.

Members of one of Barack's social groups decided to get someone from the African National Congress (ANC), an organization dedicated to increasing the rights of black Africans in South Africa, to come to their campus to speak. The reason behind such a rally was to inspire those listening in the audience to react to what they'd heard and become part of the movement to change the government's actions and policies.

Barack and his friends had planned a scene to be carried out before the ANC representative spoke. Barack was to start talking to the crowd about the wrongness of apartheid. In the middle of his speech, his friends were to come out and silence him by dragging him off the stage. This act was meant to symbolize the fact that the black Africans in South Africa didn't have a voice in their own government, and that the government did awful things to them in order to keep them quiet.

Barack began his speech: "There's a struggle going on," he said. Then, a little louder, he repeated himself. People started to pay attention. Barack noticed how his words held power, just as his father's had.

It's happening oceans away. But it's a struggle that touches each and every one of us. Whether we know it or not. Whether we want it or not. A struggle that demands we choose sides. Not between black and white. Not between rich and poor. No—it's a harder choice than that. It's a choice between dignity and

servitude. Between fairness and injustice. Between
commitment and indifference. Between right and
wrong . . .

The crowd started clapping and calling out. They wanted to know more—to hear more. Barack felt energized and ready to take the crowd on a journey with him, on a carpet woven from threads of ideas and strings of words. He could rouse their spirits. His voice carried through the air and penetrated the hearts of those in attendance. He felt he was about to change the world. Then, just as planned, two of his friends grabbed him and tried to drag him offstage. He struggled with them and tried to fight them off. It was exactly what they'd planned to do, only Barack wasn't playacting. He really wanted to stay onstage. He really felt that people were listening to him and that he could make a difference.

Instead, all the other speakers took their turns and spoke about the criminality of the South African government's practices. Some people stayed to listen, but they didn't have the same enthusiasm as before. Barack felt like a fraud.

"But **America is a great nation** precisely because **Americans** have been willing to **stand up** when it was hard; to **serve** on stages both great and small; to **rise above** moments of great challenge and terrible trial."[10]

"We now live in a
world where
the most valuable skill
you can sell is knowledge."[11]

After two years at Occidental, Barack

would write to his father again, though their communication
had all but ceased through the end of his high school and
beginning years in college. He was still searching for a sense
of belonging and was ready to find a real community where
he could lay down roots. He wanted to live among black
Americans in a setting that was not just the backdrop for a
performance like his speech. Occidental and Columbia
University in New York City had established a transfer program, where students at one could apply to finish their

schooling at the other. Barack leaped at the chance to live near the heart of Harlem, where a renaissance in black culture had occurred in the 1920s. Though the neighborhood had suffered a serious decline in prosperity since then, a large portion of the black population of New York City continued to reside there.

There was no answer at the door when he arrived at his apartment in New York in 1981. He had to sleep outside in an alleyway that night and bathe in a fire hydrant the next morning—not quite the romantic picture of inner-city life he'd painted from the stories he'd heard from his Chicagoan friend. He called a friend he knew had moved to the city, who invited him to wait in his apartment until Barack could get into his own. After many months, the two moved in together. Barack started taking better care of himself and applying himself to his studies. He cleaned up his act— though he continued smoking cigarettes—and instead started running and writing regularly in his journal. Sometimes he would play basketball on the courts in his neighborhood or listen to the Reverend Jesse Jackson speak near 125th Street.

Though Barack was discovering a lot of things in college, by living in New York City he was learning firsthand about race and class in America. He witnessed with his own eyes the disproportionate number of black people living in poor communities. Yet this wasn't South Africa, it was America! This inequality was upsetting, but what could be done?

Barack's mother and Maya came to visit in the summer

The Reverend Jesse Jackson is an American civil rights activist and prominent leader within the African-American community. He was the first black candidate to make a serious run for the Democratic presidential nomination in 1984, which he repeated in 1988, and he served as a District of Columbia "statehood senator" from 1991 to 1996. Jackson's own voter-registration drive helped Harold Washington win his election bid to become Chicago's first black mayor. Jackson is a Baptist minister and founder of the nonprofit Rainbow/PUSH Coalition (People United to Serve Humanity). He marched alongside civil rights leader Dr. Martin Luther King, Jr., and was present as a young aide when Dr. King was assassinated.

of 1982. Barack needed to make money and would work during the day at a construction site while his mom and sister would sightsee. One evening Barack asked his mom for an international stamp. He told her that he was planning to visit his dad the following year, after graduating from college. His mother sounded hopeful: She wanted the two of them to get to know each other. She told Barack something he'd never known: She had divorced his father, and that is why Barack Sr. had left them in America. She went on to explain many things about their relationship, including how both his and her parents had been unhappy about the marriage initially, Barack Sr.'s dad, Onyango, even more so. From what she understood, Onyango had written a letter to Gramps saying he objected to their union solely because she was white, and Onyango didn't want his family bloodline tainted by a white woman. Even after Barack Jr. was born, Onyango threatened to have Barack Sr.'s passport revoked.

She told Barack about his dad's choice to go to Harvard and what their first date had been like. They were young and in love—she was only eighteen when they married. He'd wanted them to return to Kenya with him after his visit when Barack was ten. But she was still married to Lolo, and Barack Sr.'s third wife had just left him. At times there was anger in her voice, but there was happiness as well. In the end, Ann admired Barack Sr. and had wanted Barack Jr. to know him through stories while he was growing up, and now she wanted him to know him in person, as an adult.

"I did not know my father well—he returned to Kenya from America when I was still young. Since that time I have known him through stories. . . ."[12]

BARACK OBAMA

Dreams from My Father
A STORY OF RACE AND INHERITANCE

"Perceptive and wise, this book will tell you something about yourself whether you are black or white."
—Marian Wright Edelman, author of *The Measure of Our Success*

"It is about the past versus the future."[13]

Barack got a phone call from Kenya.

His aunt Jane was on the line. His father, at forty-six years old, had been killed in a car accident. Barack was twenty-one.

Barack phoned his mother, who wailed into the phone. Then he dialed his father's half brother in Boston; he barely knew Omar. They spoke briefly, stiffly, and then Barack hung up. There wasn't anything left to say. Whatever answers he could have gotten or connections he could have made when he visited his dad were lost forever, sunk to the bed of an ocean somewhere between America and the African continent. Barack would not go to Kenya. Not now.

Instead he made plans for his future right here and decided he wanted to help people in black communities in the United States get back on their feet. Since the Civil Rights Movement some twenty years earlier, the black community seemed to have developed laryngitis, or else the rest of the world had gone deaf. It was time to return voices to the communities.

Barack wrote a letter of condolence to his family in Nairobi, Kenya, but he did not attend the funeral. His college classmates thought Barack's community-organizing ambitions were noble but impractical. Barack, however, was on a mission. If he could organize individuals from the base up—the grassroots—he could prove to them, and himself, his commitment to the community. He could perhaps bridge divides between those with power and those without. Whites and blacks would finally come together and unite. Perhaps, then Barack would find a place to house his split identity.

Almost a year after his father's death, Barack dreamed about his father. It was a sad dream. His father was in jail and Barack released him. His father told him he loved him, and Barack wanted them to leave the cell together, but his father wanted Barack to go by himself. Barack woke up crying. These were the first tears he'd shed since his father passed away. Somehow, someday, he would know his father and bring his story to life.

As graduation neared, Barack wrote letter after letter to community organizers and black leaders nationwide hoping to find work with them, but he got no response. Undeterred, he decided to use his degree in political science from Columbia to find work in another field for a year, during which he could pay off some student loans and save money. Then he would try again.

He was employed for a time as a research assistant at Business International Corporation (BI), where he was the only black person who wasn't a secretary, janitor, or security guard. Though Barack felt guilty for having crossed an invisible racial divide, the black secretaries were proud of him. They saw his achievements as their own and hoped what happened to him could happen in their families. The success of the one was the success of the many. When Barack told them he wanted to become a community organizer, their reactions were less enthusiastic. That job paid very little and they didn't think that, by nature, people in the community would pay attention or appreciate his efforts.

Barack got a promotion at his job, which meant he was given more responsibilities and a better salary. He started to wonder if he even needed to switch careers. He was getting used to having money and an office of his own with his own secretary. Maybe he had made it big after all and that was what mattered.

Then his half sister called. Not Maya, but Auma, his father's second child, the one born before him. She and Barack had written to each other every once in a while through the years, but they had never met or spoken before. She had been studying in Germany and was now coming to the United States, and more specifically, to New York City to visit. He insisted that she stay with him. But as soon as plans had been set, supplies purchased, and arrangements made, Auma called Barack again. She told him she wouldn't be coming. One of their brothers, David, had died in a motorcycle accident. Here was another family member Barack had not known, dead. Auma's phone call woke him up, in a manner of speaking. His desire for links to his history and community resurfaced. A few months later, he quit his job at the consulting firm and renewed his search for community-organizing work.

Gerald Kellman called. Months after Barack had turned down a community organizing gig that would have kept him in an office, instead of in the trenches where he wanted to be, he met with Gerald, who needed a trainee for his organizing drive. Gerald, who was white and Jewish, wanted to help poor people in underserved communities in Chicago, but he feared the people there wouldn't trust him since most of the community members were black. He wanted someone who could go into the black churches and get members interested and energized. The church was the heart of the community.

Gerald had a lot of experience doing this type of work. Barack had very little. Barack had tried getting a job with Harold Washington, the newly elected mayor of Chicago. But Mr. Washington, like all the other politicians, hadn't

Gramps and Toot visiting Barack in New York.

written back to him. Gerald told Barack that the city of Chicago was polarized, which meant that the white people wanted one thing and the black people wanted something else, and nobody seemed willing to negotiate or compromise. But Gerald believed that even if politicians couldn't get fair laws passed, he and his group of organizers could have a positive impact.

The job paid $10,000 the first year, and Gerald offered Barack $2,000 more so he could buy a used car (he ended up with an old Honda). The money was a fraction of what Barack had been making at BI. But this type of work, launching the Developing Communities Project (DCP) as part of the Calumet Community Religious Conference in Chicago, was what Barack had been saying he wanted to do for all these years. This was grassroots organizing at its most basic level. A week later, Barack moved from New York City to Chicago.

"And **I accepted the job,**
sight unseen,
motivated then by a single,
simple, **powerful** idea—
that **I might play**
a small part in building
a better America."[14]

"Through **words**
he gave **voice** to the voiceless.
Through **deeds**
he gave **courage**
to the faint of heart."[15]

Gerald Kellman took Barack through

the streets of Chicago to survey abandoned buildings that looked like ancient ruins from a once great civilization. At one time, people of all backgrounds worked together in those factories, though once the whistle blew at the end of the day, everyone went their separate ways and did not socialize with people from other races. Gerald understood, however, that if people wanted their jobs back, they were going to have to put their differences aside and work together.

It was going to take a long time and a lot of hard work

to get manufacturing companies to return to these areas on the South Side of Chicago. But Gerald thought people in those communities could regain a sense of hope if positive things, even little ones, started happening for them. Barack was assigned to work in the West Pullman and Roseland areas. Gerald had him read *Parting the Waters*, by Taylor Branch, which discussed the American Civil Rights Movement.

Barack began his work with the DCP by calling people on the phone to set up interviews. He wanted to know what issues were most important to them. The process reminded him of all the calls Gramps had made when he was selling insurance. The difference was, Barack believed in the value of his work. During the interviews, he found out that many individuals had grown up in self-contained black neighborhoods that sounded very much like the world his friend from Occidental College had spoken about.

However, as black people were granted rights to purchase property in predominantly white neighborhoods, white people reacted negatively, sometimes vandalizing black people's property and eventually moving away. This is sometimes called "white flight." Soon stores and banks vanished from the area as well; city services, like garbage pickup, park or street maintenance, and police protection slowed to a near standstill. The result was a decline in the quality, appearance, and value of homes and neighborhoods wherever blacks went. If their children did well in school, they tended to move away when they graduated. Poorer people then moved into the neighborhoods—those who sometimes couldn't afford the property they bought or its upkeep. This is sometimes referred to as "urban decay."

Barack learned that one major concern among parents was their children's safety. Gang activity had risen as job opportunities fell. Police didn't respond to parents' concerns. Barack discovered that many parents would be willing to participate in a meeting to address their need for police protection if one of the police district commanders in the police department would attend. Barack was excited to set up the exchange.

At least one influential church leader, however, was reluctant to encourage his congregation to participate. He didn't want to get involved in the DCP, especially when he learned it was run by someone white, namely Gerald Kellman. He needed his congregation to feel justified in mistrusting all white people. It made it easier for them to spot their enemy in their fight for justice. But the reality wasn't that simple. Since that church leader wasn't on board, other church leaders backed out too. Without church support, Barack knew the turnout at his meeting would be low. It was, and the district commander didn't even show up: He sent a community-relations officer in his place. Nothing went according to plan. The meeting failed to meet its goals. Barack was disappointed. He was going to have to find some other way to bring black people, and then white people, back to the table.

Barack took on an additional task: the Altgeld Gardens public housing project. There were two thousand apartments in a complex of two-story buildings, surrounded by the Lake Calumet landfill (another word for a dump) and the Metropolitan Sanitary District's sewage treatment plant. Needless to say, the area always stank. The families tended to take care of their apartments on the inside, but the management company in charge of the overall upkeep of the buildings was letting them crumble by not completing necessary repairs.

Unemployment was high among the residents, and the solution was not as simple as the job bank that Gerald proposed—a database of job openings that the unemployed could search. Job banks would not train workers looking for jobs in new fields or provide educations to those whose schooling had been substandard. The poorer people looking for work would not be able to take advantage of a job bank, and yet, it was the poorer people who needed the help.

One day Barack took Yvonne Lloyd (a mother of eleven children), Loretta Augustine-Herron, and another mother from the neighborhood to look for solutions to the joblessness problem at Altgeld. They had no luck at the Roseland Unity Coalition or the Chamber of Commerce. But as they were leaving the Mayor's Office of Employment and Training (MET), things started to look up. MET programs were supposed to teach people new skills that would make them more employable. No one at MET could help them that day. However, Barack noticed in their brochures that there were no MET programs anywhere near Altgeld Gardens. At last! They had found at least one source of their joblessness problem. Now they had a place to start their fight for job opportunities.

They wrote a letter to Cynthia Alvarez, the director of MET for the city. Soon they had scheduled a community meeting for her to attend in which nearly a hundred people from the region would participate. By the end of the hour-long gathering, Ms. Alvarez had made a commitment to create a MET center in a nearby area within a six-month period. It was a great achievement.

"As our parents' children,
we have the **opportunity to
learn** from these mistakes
and disappointments.
We have the **opportunity to
muster the courage** to fulfill
the **promise of our**
forefathers and **lead**
our great nations
toward **a better future.**"[16]

Barack's half sister Auma finally came

to visit him in Chicago. She told Barack that their brother
Roy now lived in Washington, D.C. Though it was their first
time meeting, Barack and Auma shared an immediate bond
as though they'd grown up together on the same continent,
in the same home. He introduced her to some of the women
he worked with, including Yvonne and Loretta, who reminded
Auma of their aunts—aunts Barack had yet to meet. Barack
told her all about his upbringing, then she told him about
Germany and what life had been like in Kenya with the

"Old Man," which is what she called their dad. She admitted that she hadn't really known him all that well. She wondered if anybody had.

Their father had returned to Kenya from the United States with a white American woman named Ruth after he'd finished studying at Harvard. Auma and Roy were going to live with him and Ruth back then, and Ruth was going to be their mother. Ruth wouldn't allow Barack Sr. to have more than one wife, and in Kenya, men got the children in a divorce. Their real mother, Kezia, hadn't had much choice but to let them go. She'd known that Barack Sr. was wealthy (relatively speaking, in terms of the life he could offer them in Kenya), so she'd come to accept that her children would be better off with him.

Barack Sr. had worked for an American oil company and had known many of the top people in Kenya's new government. He and Ruth had two sons, Mark and David. Meanwhile, Barack Sr. had continued to see his first wife, Kezia, who'd given birth to two more sons, Abo and Bernard. The Old Man had taken a job in government at the Ministry of Tourism, but by then, tribal conflicts in the country had been growing. Barack's people, the Luos, were upset that the Kikuyus, the largest tribe, had been getting all the best jobs. Though most people in government had remained quiet, Barack Sr. had spoken up. He thought that tribalism was bad for the country and that the most qualified people, regardless of their tribe, should get the best jobs. The president of Kenya, Jomo Kenyatta, eventually heard about Barack Sr.'s outspokenness and had banished him from government.

As much as he had tried, Barack Sr. couldn't find work—the Kenyan government saw to that. Eventually a friend of his had felt sorry for him and had gotten him work at the Water Department. Most people had stopped talking to him outside of work, because they were afraid the government would come after them too. Auma told Barack how their father, the Old Man, had become very bitter and started drinking a lot. Ruth had started to resent his treatment of her. After he got in a terrible car accident, she left him, leaving Roy and Auma behind. It had taken the Old Man a year to recover in the hospital. That's when, in 1971, he had gone to Hawaii to see Barack and Ann when Barack was ten.

When Barack and Ann didn't return with the Old Man as expected, things only got worse. He'd lost his job at the Water Department and he and Roy and Auma had to move to a rundown part of town. He was poor and had to borrow money from relatives. The kids essentially had been forced to raise themselves, but the Old Man had still wanted other people to believe everything was okay in his life, so he'd sometimes given what little money he had to charity. He was pretending he had more money than he actually had. Roy left home early and lived with various relatives. In time, Auma started attending Kenya High School and had been relieved not to be at home as much. After President Kenyatta died in 1978, the Old Man had been able to find work again in government in the Ministry of Finance. But he had never gotten over how he had been mistreated and shunned by his own friends.

Auma had moved to Germany and was nervous about how she and the Old Man were going to interact when he came to visit, but they had a great time. She then began to let go of some of her past disappointments. The Old Man had had another son, George, and he had seemed to agree with Auma that there was an opportunity to start fresh with him and make fewer mistakes as a father. Not too long after his visit with Auma, he was killed in a car crash. It became clear, as Auma finished telling her story to Barack, that all of the Old Man's children, every last one of them, had something in common: They had all in some way been robbed of a dad, whether they'd grown up with him in their lives or not.

"...what makes you **a man**
is not the ability
to have a child
but the **courage**
to raise one."[17]

"Instead,
Franklin Delano Roosevelt . . .
knew that, at its best,
    government can be used as
a force to accomplish
                        together
what we cannot achieve
                on our own."[18]

Auma returned to Germany. The MET, as promised, opened up an office in Roseland, near enough to Altgeld Gardens, and Mayor Harold Washington came to its grand opening. Gerald Kellman was moving to a different city that had different concerns. Barack stayed behind and Gerald reminded him that small triumphs don't amount to big changes in this world. He wanted Barack to remember that small wins were only meant to fill people with the courage to fight for bigger things.

Barack wanted to organize a group of young mothers at

Altgeld to get a few things going for the complex: toilets that flushed, heaters that worked, and so forth. One young woman approached him with a notice she'd clipped from the newspaper the day before. It stated that the Chicago Housing Authority (CHA) was looking to hire the least expensive contracting company to remove asbestos from the management offices at Altgeld. (Asbestos is a dangerous substance that was once used in building construction. People who breathe it in can become very sick from it.) Barack got the same young woman to contact the management office and ask whether there was asbestos in the apartments themselves. She was told not to worry, that testing had been performed. However, the management office couldn't provide records that showed any testing had ever been done.

After weeks of getting no proof, they decided to drive a bus to the CHA and confront the director. Yvonne and Loretta went along, as did six others. The CHA director's assistant told them there was no one around who could help them and she was going to have security remove them from the premises. Then a crowd of reporters showed up. When the assistant saw that reporters were asking about the asbestos, she brought Barack and the rest of the group into a back room. Soon Barack and the others received word that no testing had been done in the apartments but that it would be started by the end of the day. In addition, they would be granted a face-to-face meeting with the director of the CHA.

Although the meeting with the director didn't go as planned, the overall campaign had a positive outcome. The publicity from both events resulted in Altgeld receiving emergency cleanup funds from the U.S. Department of Housing and Urban Development (HUD). However, the community was given a choice: The money could go toward cleaning up the asbestos or installing new plumbing and roofing, but not both.

Barack got involved in other community-wide campaigns. In the midst of it all, he made plans to meet his half brother Roy in Washington, D.C. Roy looked different from his photos. He had gained a lot of weight, which he claimed was due to all the fast food available in America. He looked so much like his father that it surprised Barack. Unfortunately, he drove like his father as well and almost had two accidents on their way to dinner.

Roy told Barack he was probably going to get divorced. His wife thought he was behaving too much like his father, drinking too much, and so on. He recounted tales similar to the ones Auma had told Barack. But he also explained how he never felt what he did was good enough for their dad. If he got the second-best grades in school, their father would want to know why he hadn't come in first. Being the best had been a source of pride for the Old Man. He didn't want to accept any less from his children. But was their father actually the best? By then he had no money and was drinking far too often. How was that the best?

After their father died, people in the family started fighting over who would get the money and possessions he'd left behind. A lot of responsibility was left to Roy. People expected him to take care of matters like paying school fees for his half brothers and getting Auma married off. Then David died and Roy lost all hope. He and David had grown very close. His death was too much to bear. Roy started drinking and picking fights and moved to the United States—he did whatever he could to escape the pain.

Barack returned to Chicago. It was time for him to move on too. He had applied to law school so he could further his education. He'd told his high school friend Bobby Titcomb that the only way he could help people in poor neighborhoods was to have a law degree to match those of the people in power. Barack was also gravitating toward the black church because of what it meant to people in the community. For some, not belonging to the church made them feel cut off from themselves. The church was not just a place for spiritual guidance, but for receiving an education that one doesn't get in school. Black history was taught there every week, not just once a year, and African-American culture was nurtured in church. And everyone was welcome, the rich, the poor, the professional, the hooligan, because their lives were intertwined. No matter how much one wanted to be isolated from others, what one did affected everyone else. That was the lesson of the church.

Reverend Jeremiah A. Wright wrote a sermon called "The Audacity of Hope" and delivered it one Sunday morning to his congregation at the Trinity United Church of Christ. He spoke about how one must look for a glimmer of hope when all else seems lost: The light is out there, you just have to keep looking until you find it. Barack did not belong to the church then, but its messages of hope and faith in ideas bigger than himself were whispering louder and louder in his ear.

"It wasn't until **after college,
when I went to Chicago**
to work as a community
organizer for a group of
Christian churches,
that **I confronted my**
own spiritual dilemma."[19]

"The history of Africa is a history of ancient kingdoms and great traditions; the story of people fighting to be free from colonial rule; the heroism of not only great men . . . but also ordinary people who endured great hardship. . . ."[20]

Barack Obama was admitted into Harvard

Law School. But before he started, he decided to take that trip to Kenya he'd been planning for many years. He read a book on the plane about the history of African countries. Though he understood the problems that colonialism (when a country, like England or Holland, rules other nations, exploiting them for its own benefit) had inflicted upon African nations and that many Africans had fought for independence from the colonizers, Barack started to get frustrated. Many of the people on that continent were still suffering from the laws and hierarchies colonialists had instituted and left in their wake.

Barack was also nervous that he would find out that Africa, and Kenya in particular, was not his home—that he would not feel welcome there. He had spent so much time building up Kenya in his head, he was afraid he would feel let down, just as he had been let down gradually by the cracks in the mythology of his father.

When he landed, Barack could not find his suitcase. A woman who worked for the airline asked him his name. When he told her, she asked if he was related to Dr. Obama. She went on to tell him that her family had known his father well. Barack was surprised to learn that, in a nation as large as Kenya, his father's name and influence traveled far. People had known his dad and so they understood a part of him better than he did himself. That was reassuring.

Auma met Barack at the airport and introduced him to their aunt Zeituni, his father's half sister, who greeted him with the words that mean "welcome home" in Swahili. And when she left their company that first day, she made Auma promise not to let Barack get lost again. She meant that she didn't want Barack to go away for very long or lose touch with his people or family.

Auma and Barack drove to her apartment. He settled in and took a nap. When he woke up, he saw a troop of monkeys nearby. But he didn't own any of these animals, as he had in Jakarta. These monkeys roamed free.

When Auma and Barack walked through the market-place, he saw figurines like those his father had brought to him in Hawaii. Barack was also aware of the fact that he didn't stick out from the rest of the crowd. His physical characteristics were common here. No one would ask to touch his hair—it was just like theirs. He blended in and didn't have to try to justify why he belonged there or what he was doing. He would not be mistaken for a criminal because of the color of his skin. He would not be judged or asked to choose sides in a debate on race.

When he noticed American, European, and Asian tourists, however, he realized that they too felt comfortable—as though they would never feel out of place anywhere they went. They enjoyed a certain level of immunity from dislike, an untouch-ability that allowed them to feel entitled to live anyplace, hold any job, and live beyond the conflicts of these countries, whereas Barack felt permanently tied to these countries' struggles.

He walked with Auma along Kimathi Street, named after a leader of the Mau Mau rebellion—the same conflict that had troubled Toot all those years ago. When he and Auma sat down to eat, a Kenyan waiter ignored them, and never showed them the courtesy he bestowed upon nonblacks that day. It was as though the Kenyan man was filled with a self-hate that had been cultivated during the time of British rule. It was similar to what Barack saw in many African-Americans—a feeling of worthlessness that was the rule of law during slave times and appeared to be passed down from generation to generation ever since. Who really held power in Kenya now? Though Kenyans ran their government, were they still slaves to a grim belief in white racial superiority? How could they free themselves from this imprisonment of the mind?

There was a gathering at Kariako, an apartment complex, in Barack's honor. He met many of his relatives including his aunt Jane, the one who'd called him when his father was killed. He met Auma's mother, Kezia, his father's first wife. And he met Bernard, his half brother, who loved basketball almost as much as Barack. (They would play a few rounds together later in the week.) The family ate lots of different foods, like goat curry, collard greens, *ugali* (corn porridge), and fried fish, and Auma and Barack didn't leave until late that night.

Auma and Barack went back to the airport two days after his arrival to try to find his bag. The attendants weren't very helpful so the pair went to the British Airways downtown office. They were largely ignored there as well. The siblings happened upon a distant relative Auma knew. He was there to have lunch with the office manager. Once the manager learned why Barack and Auma were there, he called the airline and Barack's luggage was located within minutes. Barack realized that knowing the right people made a difference in getting things done. It was a kind of favoritism, but was it fair?

In Kenya, the commitment to family is strong. Auma brought Barack to see relative after relative. Refusing to go was not an option because Barack could not risk offending people. Additionally, people—like him—who were doing relatively well, were expected to give back to the family and share their wealth. That is what had been expected of Barack Sr., and that is what people hoped Roy and now Barack would be able to do for them, too.

Zeituni and Barack went to see his other aunt, Sarah. She had not been at the celebration due to a family feud. There had been a lot of fighting about who should inherit Barack's father's money and possessions after his death. Sarah had taken care of Barack Sr. as a child and had never gotten the advantages he did, though she was just as intelligent. She could not inherit any of their father Onyango's money since, according to custom, the male children inherited everything. So she had wanted Barack Sr. to take care of her and her child instead of Kezia and Kezia and Barack's children, whom she saw as a threat to her financial stability. She turned against them and upset Auma by stating that Auma and Roy were not Barack Sr.'s real children. That would mean only Ruth (Barack Sr.'s third wife) and her sons could inherit anything. During their brief talk, Barack noticed that Sarah seemed both desperate and bitter. She pleaded with Barack to give her some money. He did. Soon after that, he and Zeituni left.

Zeituni explained to Barack that his father had once been very generous, even to those who had turned their backs on him when the government blacklisted him and he could find no work. When he got back on his feet again, he continued to give to people who had shown him no loyalty. Zeituni thought this was a mistake. She told Barack Sr. that she thought he needed to think of himself and his family first, otherwise he would end up with nothing. She thought that if he treated everyone like family, then no one is family, because that would mean everyone would hold an equal place in his heart and no one, not even his kids, would be special and above all others. It would occur to Barack that Barack Sr., his real dad, and Lolo, his stepdad, had very different ideas about charity.

Auma reluctantly took Barack to see Ruth, Barack Sr.'s last wife, one day. Mark, her son, was home for the summer, a fuzzy image of Barack himself. He'd been studying at Stanford University in California. Ruth invited the two of them in and spent an hour measuring her son's accomplishments against Barack's. She often spoke unkindly of Barack's father, something Barack's mother, Ann, had never done.

The next day Barack met with Mark alone. Barack wondered if Mark ever wanted to return to Kenya. Mark admitted that he had only negative feelings toward their father. He chose not to think about his roots or his Kenyan side. He said he'd rather not dig deep into his past. Instead he'd live on the surface and fashion a life from a shallow knowledge of his past, which meant he'd never know if he was building an existence upon rock or quicksand. When they parted ways, it seemed clear that Barack and Mark wouldn't have much contact in the future. Oddly enough, since Ruth had papers proving that Barack Sr. was Mark's father, it was only Mark, the child who rejected his dad, who could prove his paternity and inherit his wealth, though by this time, there was not much of anything to gain.

Barack convinced Auma to go on a safari to Masai Mara, to see the animals in their natural habitats on their native continent. At dawn Barack saw them: lions lying in the grass; buffalo in the marshes; hippos; elephants, like his father had described. In the evening they saw hyenas and wildebeest. And among all the activity, there was a stillness. It was like being present at the dawn of time, in the place where man had been born from the earth. He was witnessing firsthand the stories his father had told that day in Miss Hefty's classroom.

After they returned from the safari they reunited with family, including Roy, who was back in Kenya. Barack got a fuller picture of his family by being around them and enjoying their company, and through the stories they told of the past.

Roy explained what actually happened to David, Ruth's younger son, the night he died in a motorcycle accident. David had been trying to get Roy's identification papers to free him from jail after a brawl.

Barack learned from Granny, Sarah Hussein Onyango, about how industrious his grandfather Onyango had been. He had learned about agriculture working as a servant for a British captain during World War II. At nearly fifty years old, he had started farming and had excelled at it.

Zeituni recounted the time when Onyango told a persistent man that he could only let his goat walk across their land if he kept the goat from eating, but if the goat nibbled on even half a leaf, Onyango would take its life. Of course the man couldn't keep the goat from snacking, and Onyango struck the animal dead, just as he'd warned.

And it was here in Kenya, at long last, where Barack learned his father's real nature: the fact that he'd been exceptional in school but restless and gotten kicked out, the fact that he had gotten a low-paying job but couldn't keep it, and the circumstances of how he had come to the University of Hawaii after finishing school by correspondence—that he went on a letter-writing campaign to countless universities in the United States (just as Barack had done in order to find work as a community organizer).

He learned the full reason why his grandfather had opposed Barack Sr.'s marriage to Ann—he didn't think she would return with him and be able to live as a Luo woman. And more important, he learned how to forgive his father for his absence, for his mistakes, and fully admire his strengths and perseverance despite all that life had dealt him. Barack knelt in the backyard between the gravestones of his father and grandfather and cried, releasing the pain he'd felt for not knowing all those years what they had been through, releasing the anger he had felt at his dad for not being there to guide him. Now it was time for him to rise up and let go of the stranglehold of his past. He would no longer live in a figment's shadow. His dad was real. At last he was human.

Bernard came out to get Barack and asked for a cigarette to smoke. Barack put his cigarettes away. It was time to start setting a better example for those who looked up to him, even if he would find it to be a long, difficult journey. Before he returned to America, Barack met young George, his dad's last child, on a school yard playground. In that brief introduction, he hoped to open the door for George to one day get to know his father, Dr. Barack Hussein Obama, by seeking out his larger family, just as Barack had done.

"In this country, it is **education** that **allows our children to hope** for something else."[21]

By 1988 Barack had spent four years in

Chicago and at twenty-seven he was several years older than
the average law student. But that was not what truly set him
apart from his classmates at Harvard Law School. Yes, he
had a maturity that one would expect of someone older, but
he was also very disciplined and committed to his studies.
He spent hours each day studying in the library his first
year. He got involved again in the antiapartheid movement
on campus and he wrote several articles for the school's
renowned journal, the *Harvard Civil Rights-Civil Liberties*

Law Review. It was quite a major accomplishment to be published in that periodical.

He spoke at the Black Law Students Association annual dinner and stressed the need for people like him, who had been given a lot of opportunities in life, to give back and help those who hadn't been as fortunate. He agreed with those who were clamoring for more racial diversity on the faculty.

After his first year of law school, Barack spent the summer back in Chicago, working as an intern at a law firm now known as Sidley Austin. Michelle LaVaughn Robinson worked there as an attorney and was assigned to train him. Barack liked her very much as soon as they met. Michelle, on the other hand, was skeptical of how highly others had praised Barack even before he'd gotten there. She expected him to be stuck-up, or more interested in charming people in order to move up the ranks, than in being sincere. Michelle thought it would be unprofessional to date someone she was managing. In addition, she was the only other black person at the law firm. She hated to think that people expected them to end up together—"Who else could they date?" The circumstances might sound familiar: Barack had been teased at Punahou Academy when he played with the only black girl there. But by now Barack had dated people of different races. He could choose whomever he liked. And he chose Michelle.

Michelle's family was from a predominantly African-American community on the South Side of Chicago. As children, she and her brother, Craig, had shined in different activities—he was a good student and an excellent basketball player, she was a good basketball player and an excellent student. Their home life was relatively stable, though their father, Frasier, suffered from a physical illness that affected his ability to get around. Michelle wanted to do well to make her father proud since he'd gone through so much to provide for his family. She attended Princeton University as an undergraduate (as did her brother) and had then gone on to graduate school at Harvard Law School. Her family was tight-knit, like that of Barack's Chicagoan friend whom he'd met at Occidental. The Robinsons had extended family all around and they were deeply rooted in their community.

Michelle set Barack up on a date with a friend of hers, but he wasn't interested in anyone else. After some time, she agreed to go on a date with him to Baskin-Robbins. Over chocolate ice cream, the two grew closer. After he took her to a training seminar he was conducting in the basement of a church on the South Side, and talked to a group of mainly single mothers about how to narrow the divide between the way the world is and the way it should be, Michelle fell in love with him. They were soon in a committed relationship.

Barack and Michelle continued dating even after he returned to Harvard. Throughout the remainder of his time there, he fine-tuned his powers of persuasion and proved himself capable of helping people on opposite sides of an issue reach a reasonable compromise. He became an editor for *Harvard Law Review* and eventually his friends convinced him to run for president of the publication in 1990. At that time people on the review were either fiercely liberal (meaning they thought there was a lot of progress yet to be made in society on issues such as civil rights and gender equality, and believed that the government needed to step in to force progress along, as it did during the Civil Rights Movement), or they were considered fiercely conservative (meaning they were opposed to that type of change, especially through governmental laws, and even believed that the government had done too much to force social change and should reverse some laws). Barack was clearly liberal-minded, but he was also open-minded. He always listened to both sides of an issue before forming his own conclusion. Conservative people appreciated this aspect of his personality and during elections for president of the *Law Review,* those conservatives, who had no chance of winning on their own, decided to support Barack over David Goldberg because they knew, even if Barack disagreed with their position, he would at least consider it.

While president of the journal, Barack was faced with a difficult task: He could only give a few of the seventy-five people who were part of the organization larger roles in helping to run it. He believed African Americans, women, and other minorities deserved more of a voice on the staff than they'd been given in the past, but he also thought that people who were qualified shouldn't be passed over for positions just because they were white men. He ultimately selected a diverse group of people and gave them leadership positions, which upset many black participants, who believed he should have placed more of an emphasis on including them in order to make up for the years in which blacks were all but excluded. Despite their disappointment, the journal under Barack's watch ran smoothly and people came to see him as fair-minded and practical.

Barack Obama was the very first black individual to become president of the *Harvard Law Review*. Many agreed it was a long time coming, and when news of the achievement reached the local press, he was asked by a publisher to write a book about the details of his unusual upbringing and hard-earned success. In addition, high-end law firms across the country were beating down his door, trying to get him to join their firms.

One such suitor was Judson H. Miner, from the law firm of Miner, Barnhill & Galland. When Miner contacted the *Law Review* office, he was told he was number 647 on the list of people who wanted to offer Barack work. Much to Miner's surprise, Barack did choose to join his firm, largely because it was in Chicago, where Barack was finding his footing near Michelle, and also because the firm worked with victims of discrimination and civil rights abuses. Barack also liked the fact that Miner had been one of the lawyers hired by Harold Washington, the first black mayor of Chicago, to fight the city council as Washington tried to uplift the downtrodden black neighborhoods there. Barack graduated from Harvard Law School in 1991.

"Some of it has to do with the trajectory of his life. In his rise from poverty, his self-study and ultimate mastery of language and of law, in his capacity to overcome personal loss and remain determined in the face of repeated defeat—in all of this we see a fundamental element of the American character, a belief that we can constantly remake ourselves to fit our larger dreams."[22]

CHAPTER
FOURTEEN

Barack and Michelle continued their
courtship in Chicago, but Barack didn't go to work for
Miner right away. Instead he spent six months fulfilling a
commitment he'd made to work on a voter-registration
drive, a decision he'd made before accepting the job with
Miner. Project Vote was intended to help those who'd never
voted in the past come to understand the election process
and register to vote in time to participate in the upcoming
1992 United States presidential elections. Barack ran the
Illinois Project Vote campaign, which managed to get one

hundred and fifty thousand people registered. This effort helped presidential candidate William Jefferson Clinton win Illinois over George Herbert Walker Bush. Carol Moseley Braun, a representative on the state level in the Illinois General Assembly, was elected at the same time to the United States Senate—the first African-American woman to be so. In the midst of all this, Barack was teaching constitutional law at the University of Chicago in the evenings and working hard on writing his memoirs late at night, which left Michelle feeling lonely. But Michelle was an outspoken woman, and as she learned to live with the occasional time apart, she also reminded Barack to pay more attention to his personal life.

Barack and Michelle were married by Reverend Jeremiah A. Wright on October 18, 1992 at Trinity United Church of Christ in Chicago. Barack continued to work at the law firm but grew antsy to affect more change for a larger number of people. In 1995, when Alice Palmer, a state senator in the Illinois General Assembly, decided to run for a seat in the U.S. Congress, Barack decided to try to win her vacant spot in state government in Illinois's Thirteenth District. She supported him for the Democratic nomination, as they believed in similar causes. But when Palmer's election campaign started to go badly and it was clear she wasn't going to win a seat in the House of Representatives, she wanted her seat back in the state senate.

Many high-ranking black officials thought Barack should step aside and wait his turn. He had time to look for another opportunity to run, whereas Alice was already an elected official and she couldn't afford to be out of public office for any length of time if she wanted to further her career. But by then, Barack had begun campaigning and didn't want to drop out. He was ambitious and sometimes impatient. Palmer had a lot of established leaders behind her and in order to be able to run in the state senate elections, she needed her supporters to sign a petition encouraging her reelection bid. She submitted a petition of one hundred supporters quickly, which Barack thought was fishy. He didn't understand how she could have gotten it done so fast. So he challenged the petition, which, as it turns out, did not have enough valid supporter signatures on it, and Palmer could no longer continue in the race. Barack got the nomination and went on to win the election easily, representing a predominantly Democratic district.

Meanwhile, on November 7, 1995, Stanley Ann Dunham passed away after an extended battle with ovarian cancer. She had been living in Hawaii near her mother, worrying how she could afford all her medical bills while trying to convince her children, Maya and Barack, now grown adults, that life was not ending for any of them. Barack was in the beginning of his campaign and was not with her when she passed away, which is his life's biggest regret. Ann was cremated and Barack and Maya released her ashes over the water on the South Shore of Oahu, Hawaii.

Although some black politicians and community

members didn't like how Alice Palmer had been forced from the race, the Black Caucus leader, Emil Jones, Jr., became close with Barack. He encouraged Dan Shomon, an excellent staff member, to work with Barack. Shomon suggested Barack tour other parts of Illinois to get to know people outside of Chicago, if Barack ever intended to run for higher political office. Barack found he got along with the people in the rural parts of downstate Illinois. They were mostly white and middle-class. What was especially encouraging was that they took a liking to him too, even though the people in those areas had a history of being racially intolerant, especially during the Civil Rights Movement. But they reminded Barack of his grandparents and he felt he understood them well. They tended to agree.

The Illinois General Assembly was made up of more Republicans than Democrats. In general, when that happens it is difficult for Democrats to pass laws that are important to their constituents.

In his first and second terms in the state legislature, Barack got fourteen laws passed each year, and in his third year, eleven of the sixty bills he introduced or cosponsored became laws. Barack was this successful as a young politician in the minority party because he didn't exclude Republicans when he drafted his plans. He had learned from his days as president of the *Harvard Law Review* how to work with people with opposing views. Eventually he became chairman of the Health and Human Services Committee.

Barack managed to get a variety of laws passed, many with bipartisan support: a prostate-screening initiative funded by the state (prostate cancer is a disease that affects many men, a significant proportion of them African American); increased funding for a) after-school programs, b) the removal of lead from homes, and c) AIDS prevention programs; health care access for low-income families; increased scrutiny of racial profiling by police; and a law that required police to videotape their interrogations of murder suspects (so their convictions would be less likely to be overturned by appeals courts and so it would be less likely that the wrong people were sentenced to death). His bill on campaign finance reform succeeded: People running for election were no longer allowed to ask for money from anyone while they were at work (in essence, on state property), nor were lawmakers allowed to accept gifts from people with self-serving agendas or who wanted favors in return (like lobbyists or underhanded contractors).

Michelle Obama gave birth to their first daughter, Malia (which means "calm" in Hawaiian and "queen" in Swahili), in 1999. Barack's family was growing, but he was still committed to achieving his political goals. Instead of running for mayor against a very powerful opponent, Richard

M. Daley, he decided that Bobby Rush, a black politician who had been a leader of the Black Panther Party in Illinois, was not the strongest candidate and could therefore be challenged in the Democratic primary for his seat in the House of Representatives. Rush had admitted that the gun-toting he had advocated as a Black Panther did more damage than good within the community he was trying to protect, but the younger Obama had only worked on the South Side of Chicago for a few years. Did that compare to someone who had made a name for himself during the Civil Rights Movement in the 1960s?

Some people, perhaps Rush's own political advisors, outwardly began to question whether Barack was "black enough" to represent this mostly black district—whether his priorities were in line with theirs. And whether his white parentage somehow made him less authentic as a black man. Barack managed to get some donations to his campaign, but he didn't raise nearly enough money to be able to advertise on television. Rush also had a lot of credibility with blacks, even though he hadn't made a huge impact in Congress. Barack had been raised in Hawaii and attended Punahou Academy, Columbia University, and Harvard University— what some would call elite, expensive, private institutions. Rush billed himself as homegrown and authentic, having grown up—and attended college—in Chicago. Things were not looking good for Barack.

Rush's son was killed on October 18, 1999—gunned down. Whether or not it was a case of mistaken identity (one of the killers said he thought Huey was carrying money for a drug dealer), it was a tragedy and no one, not even Rush's opponent, Obama, could get away with criticizing him at that time. Meanwhile, while 90 percent of the people in the first Congressional district recognized Bobby Rush's name, 11 percent or fewer knew who Barack was. Later, Barack missed an important vote on Governor George Ryan's Safe Neighborhoods Act, a gun control law. Barack had been in Hawaii with his family during the December holiday season. Michelle was upset that Barack had been spending so much time away from his family while he was campaigning. Barack decided to stay longer in Hawaii when Malia got sick and ended up missing the vote. Though Barack generally had a high voting record, few accepted his reason for missing this one. *The Chicago Tribune* dismissed it as well. Barack's campaign could not recover from these events and was defeated in the election by thirty percentage points—a rout.

"... In the end,
neither policy nor politics
can replace heart
and courage in the struggle
you now face. Because
in the brief history of
the American experiment,
it has been the ability of
ordinary Americans to act
on both that has
allowed our nation to achieve
extraordinary things."[23]

The year was 2001, and Barack and his

family were now in debt because he had financed some of his campaign using his credit card (his camp had only managed to raise a meager $535,000 in campaign contributions), and he and Michelle both had student loans to pay. Barack was not a man driven by personal wealth—that was not how he had been raised.

Barack and Michelle welcomed a second daughter, Sasha (Natasha), into their lives that year, and it was time for Barack to slow down a bit, build a stable home environment, and spend more time with his family. Barack went back to work in the General Assembly with an added layer of humility and a commitment to getting things done on a smaller scale. Those black officials who had criticized his run against Bobby Rush found themselves working with a humbled man who was trying to mend fences. Barack got a lot done in the eight years he spent in state government, including getting nearly two hundred and eighty bills passed.

On September 11, 2001, America was attacked by Muslims from the extremist group Al Qaeda. Barack Obama's name sounded like a Muslim one, and there was prejudice brewing in America against all people of that faith because of the acts of the few hate-filled and vicious individuals among them. It seemed as though Barack's dreams of ever holding higher political office in America were over.

Then, in 2002, it became clear that an Illinois politician, the Republican senator Peter Fitzgerald, was going to have a tough time getting reelected in the United States Senate. Even members of his own party were not pleased with his performance in Congress. Barack's ambitions to do more on a larger stage began to nag at him again. He still needed to prove that he could succeed, even where his father could not. Barack wanted to make something positive and sturdy come of his unstable past. He had something to prove to his dad, to those who thought his promising career was over after his loss to Rush, and to himself.

What made this particular seat in the senate especially attractive to Barack was that it was held by a Republican whose party controlled both houses of Congress at the time. The party whose members hold the most seats usually gets to call the shots in passing legislation. Picking up an additional seat for the Democratic party would be a great win for Democrats.

The problem with this plan was that there was another Democrat who was thinking about running against the Republican. Carol Moseley Braun had lost her seat to Fitzgerald four years earlier and was thinking she might like to win it back. Barack put out feelers among his fellow Illinois senate colleagues, many of whom seemed to approve of the idea of his running. Barack had to see if his wife felt the same way. She remained practical and kept a sense of humor about it. She knew they could hardly afford another campaign, especially if he were to lose. Barack told her he would write a good book to help with the expenses, which Michelle thought was far-fetched. Still, she gave him his blessing and they planned to take out a second mortgage on their apartment.

Carol Moseley Braun decided not to run for the senate seat and instead run for president of the United States. This was the last bit of encouragement that Barack needed. He knew he was going to need ten million dollars in campaign money to have a good shot of winning the election. He called up David Axelrod, a campaign consultant and strategist, who happened to be looking for a politician to help out. Meanwhile, President George W. Bush was looking to go to war with Iraq, under what proved to be a false claim that the country had "weapons of mass destruction" that could wipe out entire nations if they were used. Many Americans, including members of Congress, were still feeling afraid because of what had occurred on September 11, 2001, and they believed the president and his cabinet, Vice President Richard B. Cheney, Secretary of Defense Donald Rumsfeld, Secretary of State Colin Powell, and National Security Advisor Condoleezza Rice, who all had made the case to go to war. Vice President Cheney even suggested that Saddam Hussein, the dictator and leader of Iraq, another Muslim nation in the Middle East, had been involved in either the planning or execution of those terrorist attacks on America. This turned out to be completely untrue.

United Nations weapons inspectors, who were searching for but could not find any weapons of mass destruction, had been kicked out of Iraq by the dictator, and the United States insisted that Saddam Hussein let the inspectors back into the country. Hussein refused to allow it, so the president asked Congress to allow him to go to war with Iraq if Hussein did not back down. Barack Obama did not think it was wise to rush to war and delivered a speech on October 2, 2002 at an antiwar rally in Chicago, where he said just that. It was a risky stance to take, as a majority of Americans and Republicans believed President Bush when he linked Saddam Hussein with both the September 11 attacks and weapons of mass destruction. Congress authorized President Bush to go to war with Iraq. Though Saddam Hussein had relented and said the inspectors could return, America started a war in Iraq on March 20, 2003.

"The answer is, with the right leadership, we can."[24]

There was a crowded field of Democrats

in 2004 who wanted to run for the second Illinois senate seat beside Senator Dick Durbin in Congress. Of the seven, Blair Hull was the wealthiest businessman who could spend millions of his own money in the race; therefore, he was Barack's major concern. Barack sought to shore up his base support of African Americans and liberal-leaning party officials, including the Reverend Jesse Jackson. Barack still had to win back support from black voters after trying to unseat the popular Bobby Rush. His work as a community organizer and the laws he trumpeted in the Illinois General Assembly were solid proof that he cared about their concerns. Their lingering doubts about whether he truly spoke for them were all but washed away. White voters liked the fact that Obama's mother was from Kansas, his grandfather had worked on oil rigs, and that Barack had gone to elite schools, culminating in his stint as president of the *Harvard Law Review*. Barack seemed to be the whole package.

Hull lost a lot of support for his campaign when some messy details about his divorce came out. Barack had other opponents to contend with, but his staff was getting things right. David Axelrod created television commercials for Barack that showed him in a very positive light. "Yes, we can" was the message that viewers came away with and started to believe. Barack hadn't liked the slogan initially because it was so simple, but he let those with more experience make the final decision. In the end, it paid off. People started to hope that "Yes, we can" change the course of American politics and improve lives, including our own. On primary night, Barack won 95 percent of the black vote, though he had started out his campaign with just 15 percent, and he won 53 percent of votes overall. The results were more than anyone had imagined possible. "Yes, we can! Yes, we can!" the crowd roared during his postelection party. It was a victory unlike any other, but it was bittersweet. Barack knew that he could very well be elected to the senate, and if he were, he would see his daughters even less.

The only thing standing in Barack's way for the senate seat was Republican Jack Ryan. Jack's campaign seemed doomed from the start. He had a field tracker, Justin Warfel, follow Barack everywhere he went, videotaping his every move, which annoyed Barack. One day Barack introduced the man to the journalists in the state capitol press room as his "stalker." The journalists couldn't believe the man wouldn't leave Barack alone and several papers ran stories about it the next day. Ryan's people had to apologize to Barack. Ryan stayed in the race for several more months despite this event and a divorce scandal of his own. But Republicans decided they needed to replace Ryan with someone who might stand a better chance against Obama.

Meanwhile, John Kerry, who was about to win the Democratic presidential nomination, decided that he wanted Barack Obama to give the keynote speech at the Democratic National Convention. This was a huge honor, as several politicians Barack admired had delivered that address in the past, including former presidential candidate Jesse Jackson, former president Bill Clinton, and the former governor of New York Mario Cuomo. This was an especially important presidential election, because George W. Bush was trying to hang on to the presidency for four more years. He had taken the country to war in Iraq without any idea how long it would last or how to end it. In addition, the United States had lost international support for the war, among other Bush policies. Sandra Day O'Connor was also likely to retire from the Supreme Court, so the next president would be able to decide her replacement. With all these issues at stake, the direction of the country hung in the balance.

Because the keynote speech wasn't going to be televised live on the major broadcast television networks, Barack had a lot more control over what he would say. He decided his speech would be about his upbringing and his hope for a united America, where everyone had a common goal that could be reached by helping one another out. He spoke before 5,000 delegates. Everyone in the room was won over instantly. It was considered one of the finest speeches in recent history. Afterward, contributions to Barack's campaign swelled by $14 million.

Back in Illinois, the Republicans decided that Obama's racial identity was working in his favor in his campaign for senator, and that it would be difficult to politically assault him based on his race. So they imported a black candidate of their own, Alan Keyes. Keyes was from Maryland, but the Republicans wanted to see if pitting a black candidate against a black candidate would somehow make Barack more vulnerable to criticism. Keyes was extremely conservative in his views, and although Barack had worked with conservatives before, he was amazed at how Keyes attacked him and questioned whether he was a true Christian. Keyes's negativity didn't appeal to Illinois voters and he never really stood a chance against Obama. Keyes won only 29 percent of the vote while Obama finished with 70 percent. This did not come as a surprise to anyone at the time.

Just as he promised his wife he would, Barack received another publishing contract in December 2004. This time he would write three books, including a children's book with his wife, Michelle. He had done all he had set out to do.

Barack's keynote speech about his upbringing and his hope for America at the 2004 Democratic National Convention in Boston is considered by many to have brought him into the national spotlight.

"Change is never easy,

but always possible."[25]

"But **elections are not enough.**
In a true **democracy,**
it is what happens between
elections that is **the true
measure** of how a
government **treats its
people.**"[26]

Senator Barack Obama took the oath of

office in January 2005; then he, Michelle, Malia, and Sasha walked outside in the direction of the Library of Congress. Malia, who was six at the time, asked her father if he was going to be president. It was a sweet moment, but it also made Barack a little uncomfortable. He had work to do in the senate, and he didn't want to rub his new colleagues the wrong way by seeming too ambitious.

Being a member of the United States Senate was not going to be easy. Barack was a low-ranking member by anyone's standards, coming in 99 out of 100 in terms of seniority. He was only the fifth black person ever elected to the United States Senate, but that didn't matter on the floors of Congress.

Barack's political team decided they needed a plan for his first two years in office. They wanted him to be a strong candidate when the 2008 elections came around, so that someone running for president of the country might consider choosing him to be his or her vice president, or perhaps Barack might be in the position to run for president himself.

So Barack held nearly forty town-hall meetings back in his home state of Illinois in order to listen to the concerns of his constituents and make sure he addressed their needs on Capitol Hill. He also did a fair amount of traveling to many different countries as a member of the Foreign Relations Committee, including Russia, the Middle East, and Iraq where, two years later, America was still at war. He tried not to make too many political waves. On top of all this, Barack had a book to write. His family stayed in Illinois and he rented an apartment in Washington D.C. He returned to Illinois on Fridays and spent Sundays with his family.

Barack could not expect to get a lot of bills passed at work. His party was in the minority. But he had already faced this type of politics in the Illinois General Assembly before his party had regained control. Instead of griping, Barack again looked to cooperate with members of the Republican party, as theirs was the party in control. This didn't always sit well with Democrats, but Barack had learned time and again that it was the only way to get things done.

Obama's fellow Democrats were annoyed that, two weeks into his term, he voted with Republicans to limit the amount of money that could be awarded to plaintiffs in class-action lawsuits (when a group of people sue a large corporation for money because of something the corporation has done to cause them injury). But Barack defended his position, because he believed that the people who were injured often didn't receive real or significant compensation for their losses. On the other hand, sometimes cases were settled too quickly before going to trial. When this happened, no one ever learned who was really to blame because the companies, fearing that juries would award sums bigger than they could afford, would settle preemptively, whether or not they were to blame.

Barack cosponsored a bill in May with Republican senator John McCain from Arizona and Democrat senator Edward (Ted) Kennedy from Massachusetts on the Secure America and Orderly Immigration Act. They hoped to find a way to control illegal immigration into the United States, but the bill was defeated in the House of Representatives. He worked with Senator Tom Coburn, a staunch conservative Republican, on several bills, including the Federal Funding Accountability and Transparency Act, which allows Americans to see online how their tax dollars are spent; they also got unanimous senate approval of the

OVERSEE Act, designed to limit favoritism in awarding reconstruction contracts in the relief efforts after Hurricane Katrina broke the levees and destroyed parts of New Orleans, Louisiana. Though many Americans were outraged at the government's handling of the rescue-and-relief effort after the hurricane, African Americans saw the government's apathy as being clouded by a racial lens, since most of the victims were black.

Rapper Kanye West had gained a lot of attention for stating on live television that President George W. Bush didn't care about black people. Barack went on television and spoke with host George Stephanopoulos. He acknowledged black Americans had a mistrust of the government, due to its historical and recent treatment of the community, but he saw the government's failure more along economic lines. He thought that those in charge in the Department of Homeland Security didn't understand the poverty of that community nor could they fathom how the poverty in the Ninth Ward had left the victims unable to escape. (The president himself had congratulated the head of the department for doing a good job in the midst of the chaos, apparently ignorant of the extent of the devastation.) However, Barack also acknowledged that because black Americans were disproportionately poorer due to how they had been treated throughout America's history, race and class (economics) were, for the time being, inextricably linked. His tempered speech helped to tone down the racial tensions that had risen after the government's failure to rescue those in need in Louisiana. Barack would later give the commencement address to the graduates of Xavier University in New Orleans in early August 2006.

One could argue Barack's most significant legislative feat was teaming up with Senator Richard Lugar of Indiana on a fact-finding mission in 2005 to Russia, Azerbaijan, and Ukraine. They were looking for stockpiles of weapons from the former Soviet Union. The Lugar-Obama Act was aimed at increasing the ability of the State Department to help the former Soviet Union find and forbid the production or stockpiling of those weapons. President Bush signed the bill into law in January 2007.

Barack traveled with his family to Africa in 2006. He was tired after completing his book *The Audacity of Hope*. He had also spread himself thin with his senatorial and familial duties. He was smoking again due to the stress of it all. Still, he soldiered on. They first arrived in South Africa, the country that had once nurtured the system of apartheid. Now there were black leaders like Bishop Desmond Tutu in power, many of whom had spent almost two decades in prison for trying to fight that injustice. Barack had begun his political career on college campuses in a fight against apartheid. He was glad to see how that part of the world had changed because everyday people there and across the globe had not given up the fight. Barack was a relative unknown in South Africa, except among the American reporters who followed him around on his trip. It was a rare period of anonymity that he would experience.

Barack and his grandmother, Sarah (Granny)
during his trip to Kenya in 2006.

The family then traveled to Nairobi, Kenya, where Barack was treated like a Hollywood celebrity. He met state officials for private lunches, and Kenyans would leave work early to catch a glimpse of the lost son who had finally returned home.

Barack and his wife, Michelle, took voluntary HIV tests because there was an AIDS epidemic coursing about the African continent. By then one in five African people had been infected with the disease. AIDS is not curable, though drugs do exist that can slow the progression of the disease. Unfortunately, most Africans could not get access to those drugs for a variety of reasons, both economic and political. Barack and Michelle took the test to try to show African people and their leaders that there was no shame in finding out whether one was infected. Having that knowledge meant people could take steps to keep from getting infected or find ways to get treatment and prevent its spread.

His family also traveled to the village in Kogelo where Barack's extended family lived. Reporters tagged along as he introduced his family to Granny. Auma, his half sister, was there too. Though Barack had planned to visit the gravesite of his father and grandfather, there was too much media surrounding him for him to have any privacy.

Barack spoke to a group of students and professors at the University of Nairobi about Kenyan politics. The fanfare he had received in the streets was not present in the university setting, where people wanted him to speak specifically about how to end political corruption in Kenya.

Still, Barack Obama was an international hit, drawing respect and admiration from audiences the world over. He would return home more convinced than ever that he had what it took to run for the presidency of the United States.

"America will rise again.
And hope will rise again."[27]

"But I have asserted a firm conviction—a conviction rooted in my faith in God and my faith in the American people—that working together we can move beyond some of our old racial wounds, and that in fact we have no choice if we are to continue on the path of a more perfect union."[28]

Barack Obama threw his hat into the

ring. On February 10, 2007, he announced in Springfield,
Illinois, that he would be running for president of the United
States. It was a big leap. He hadn't served out his full six-
year term as a U.S. senator, yet felt he was ready to lead the
nation that leads the world. As in every race he'd run, he
first had to win the Democratic nomination, and he was not
alone in his ambition: Representative from the Tenth District of Ohio Dennis Kucinich; Governor Bill Richardson of
New Mexico; former U.S. senator from North Carolina and

Democratic vice presidential nominee John Edwards; former first lady and current U.S. senator from New York Hillary Rodham Clinton; U.S. senator from Delaware Joe Biden; U.S. senator from Connecticut Christopher Dodd; former governor of Iowa Thomas Vilsack; and former U.S. senator from Alaska Mike Gravel all wanted the same spot. Some people thought Barack was jumping the gun and should wait his turn.

In the beginning, few people were counting on Barack Obama to make a significant impact in the race. People like former senator John Edwards and Senator Clinton seemed to be the obvious choices to win the nomination. Edwards had spent the years since he and John Kerry lost in 2004 campaigning in Iowa, the first state during the primary season that gets to choose the candidate it would like to run on the Democratic ticket. Hillary Clinton had the backing of her husband, former president Bill Clinton, who was still very popular among Democrats. In addition, the two had been in politics in the country's capital since 1992. They knew everyone.

Barack requested Secret Service protection in May of 2007, the earliest any candidate had ever received it, though Hillary Clinton had been under their protection since her days as first lady. The request was not made as a result of any detailed threat on his life, but perhaps because of general threats being made. In publicized debates, Edwards, Clinton, and Obama continuously stood out as reasonable choices for the nomination, so the remainder of the candidates eventually dropped out of the race.

Oprah Winfrey was one of Barack's early supporters.

Barack received the endorsement of Governor Bill Richardson, a superdelegate and prominent Hispanic politician.

Senator Barack Obama and Senator Hillary Rodham Clinton. The 2008 presidential election will make history!

But it was Barack Obama who was raising the most money and attracting the most new donors. Oprah Winfrey, the influential talk-show host, philanthropist, and business-woman, decided to use her sway with the American public and campaign for him. Whenever figures were released on how much money each campaign had raised, Obama's or Clinton's camp was on top in the Democratic contest and they were also beating the Republicans. Obama's fund-raising depended on small donations from many individuals (often over the Internet), versus large donations from fewer individuals (which is how Senator Clinton and Senator McCain, the likely Republican nominee, raised a majority of their funds). Hillary Clinton had raised $26 million the first quarter to Barack's $25 million, but in the second quarter, Barack raised $32.5 million to Hillary's $27 million.

Barack Obama won a Grammy on February 10, 2008, for "Best Spoken Word Album" for the audio version of his book *The Audacity of Hope: Thoughts on Reclaiming the American Dream*. He beat out former presidents Jimmy Carter and Bill Clinton, husband of Barack's Democratic presidential primary rival, Hillary Rodham Clinton. This was his second Grammy. He won his first in 2005 for the audio version of *Dreams from My Father*.

The campaign itself would follow a similar yo-yo pattern. To everyone's surprise, Obama won the Iowa caucus, somewhat derailing Senator Edwards (who came in second) and disappointing Senator Clinton, who had decided to be competitive there yet came in third. But Clinton bounced back in the next primary in New Hampshire, where Obama came in second.

State by State Results

With each state primary or caucus, the candidates were awarded a share of the state's delegates, people who would pledge their support for their candidate at the Democratic National Convention in Denver from August 25 through 28 of 2008. That proportion of delegates was somewhat based on how many people voted for each candidate in total—the "popular" vote. Superdelegates were members of the party who could vote for anyone they wanted at the convention, regardless of how their state voted. The democratic nominee had to win at least 2,024 out of 4,047 delegates in order to be declared the winner. Jan. 3: IA Obama. Jan. 8: NH Clinton. Jan. 15: MI Clinton, though as of now their primary results don't count because Michigan broke Democratic National Committee rules and held its primary too early; in addition, Obama was not even on the ballot. Jan. 9: NV Clinton, though Obama got one more delegate. Jan. 26: SC Obama. Jan. 29: FL Clinton, though no one campaigned there and votes did not count because Florida also broke DNC rules and held its primary too early. SUPER TUESDAY, Feb. 5: AL Obama; AK Obama; AZ Clinton; AR Clinton; CA Clinton; CO Obama; CT Obama; DE Obama; GA Obama; ID Obama; IL Obama; KS Obama; MA Clinton; MN Obama; MO Obama; NJ Clinton; NM Clinton; NY Clinton; ND Obama; OK Clinton; TN Clinton; UT Obama. Feb 9: LA Obama; WA Obama; NE Obama. Feb 10: ME Obama. Feb 12: DC Obama; MD Obama; VA Obama. Feb 19: HI Obama; WI Obama. March 4: OH Clinton; RI Clinton; TX Clinton; VT Obama. Mar 8: WY Obama. Mar 11: MS Obama.

A lot was made of this primary race across the world because, after Edwards dropped out, it was clear that, for the first time in history, a woman or a black person would be the Democratic presidential nominee. That had never happened before in America. As the campaign wore on, each side tried not to use gender or race as the reason why he or she should gain support or allies or win the nomination. Obama drew crucial endorsements from prominent and influential Democrats, including former candidate Christopher Dodd and former presidential candidate Senator John Kerry. He also managed to win the endorsement of the second longest-serving senator, Democrat Edward Kennedy, and his niece Caroline Kennedy, who saw in Obama the same grace, skill, and leadership potential that people had seen in her father, John F. Kennedy.

Campaigns need to raise a lot of money in order to get their messages out to the most people. They want to advertise on television, which costs upwards of $2,000 for 30 seconds of airtime during newscasts. They also want to travel to all the states in the Union and speak to voters at different events. Candidates travel with several people, like speech writers and campaign advisers, all of whom need to rent hotel rooms wherever they go. A typical presidential campaign can cost more than $200 million, from start to finish.

Campaigns often get heated, and this one was no exception. Senator Clinton's judgment in voting to authorize the now unpopular Iraq war was called into question, as was Barack's inexperience in Washington, D.C. Clinton's hurdle seemed a steeper one to climb, as most Democrats by 2008 were tired of the war and disheartened by its lack of progress. Obama's skills in the state senate as well as his commanding presence and the boldness and sincerity of his speeches drew large numbers of Democrats and Independents into his corner.

The press would learn in March 2008 that earlier in the year, contractors in President Bush's State Department had looked at the passport records of Senators Clinton, Obama, and McCain without permission (three times in Obama's case). This is a breach of security at one of the highest levels of government and is against the law. Two state department officials were fired. It is unclear what the violators' intentions were in committing these illegal acts or how they received such access. But it is disturbing because it is an invasion of privacy and such information could be used to spy on candidates or commit worse acts against them. These files contain people's addresses, social security numbers, and other sensitive information.

When Obama won the South Carolina primary, former president Bill Clinton demeaned the triumph on January 26 by saying that Jesse Jackson had won there in 1984 and 1988 when Jackson ran for president. Many believe that Bill Clinton was suggesting that South Carolina's large African-American population had helped these two candidates win there just because they were black, but that such a win was insignificant in the grand scheme of things. (Jackson won only five states in his 1984 presidential bid and eleven in 1988, but he was the first African-American to win any state primary.) Racial identity had been dragged back into the conversation. It was something that Obama had been trying to rise above. He saw himself not as a black candidate, but as a person running for president who happened to be black.

Other prominent politicians who favored Hillary Clinton made similar divisive statements. Geraldine Ferraro, the first female Democratic vice presidential nominee in 1984, claimed that if Barack had been white or a woman, he would not be enjoying the support he currently was.

In both cases, Obama managed to ignore the racist edge to these assertions and concentrated instead on ways to positively spin his message of bringing change to America and American politics.

But then videos of his pastor, Reverend Jeremiah A. Wright, began to surface on television and on video Web sites, like YouTube. Wright, who had served in the Marines and Navy in the 1960s and received three letters of commendation from the White House, was the head of Obama's church and a close friend of Obama's, but he had made very negative, divisive comments about America and white society. People began to wonder how Obama could consider a man with such anger toward white society a friend and confidant. Wright had, after all, baptized Malia and Sasha, and it was his sermon on the audacity of hope that had drawn Barack to the Christian faith. People, especially white people in the press, began to confuse Wright's generalizations and views about whites with Obama's.

Obama could have let the controversy blow over as he had the Bill Clinton and Ferraro remarks, and he would likely have continued to move easily toward the Democratic nomination. After all, he had won more of the popular vote than Hillary Clinton, he had more pledged delegates in his corner, and he was picking up superdelegates at a rapid pace. But this one issue struck him at his core and stuck with him. Despite the fact that his aides wanted him to keep quiet and let it blow over, he knew he had to speak the truth about race in American society—the truth he had lived his entire life, torn between two cultures seemingly at constant odds with each other. He was the legacy of both worlds. It would be the most important speech of his political career.

He delivered his speech "A More Perfect Union," at the Constitution Center in Philadelphia on March 18, 2008. Barack explained to white people that his pastor had grown up during a time when black people were not allowed to hold certain jobs, have pensions, or get good educations— our government had created laws whose purpose was to keep the black community poor and without hope for progress, while at the same time ensuring that white people routinely maintained a financial edge over blacks. Many black people had not been able to rise out of the poverty the government had inflicted upon them through hundreds of years of slavery and decades of Jim Crow laws, and many black people still suffered today in low-income, desperate, crime-ridden communities because of it. Black people of his pastor's generation had a mistrust of American government. They sometimes lashed out at entire ethnic communities, which they blamed for injuring them physically, psychologically, or both. They turned their despair outward and it manifested itself as hate. Very often, their anger was misdirected, but it was born from true disadvantages. White people needed to understand that black people's wariness was justified and their concerns were real, not imagined.

Likewise, black people needed to understand that white people and immigrants of later generations didn't feel tied to that past. They were trying to make ends meet themselves. They were trying to get ahead and were struggling to keep their own jobs. It was for this reason that they might feel resentment when the government looked to help historically disadvantaged people over them, when they were not and had never been actively involved in the racist treatment of blacks.

Barack reminded Americans that what was keeping everyone down was the fact that workers were losing their jobs to people in other countries, because American businesses wanted to pay less for labor. In addition, people running the businesses were in the habit of paying themselves a lot, while leaving ordinary Americans behind, scraping to get by. There existed a culture of corruption in politics and business, where greed overruled decency and fairness. All Americans were struggling and worried about their financial future, and all Americans, regardless of their backgrounds, needed to understand why people on the other sides of the divides were bitter or in pain.

The speech was hailed nationally and globally as groundbreaking, honest, and historic. Some labeled it the most significant speech of an entire generation. But Barack might have paid a price, because America has always been uncomfortable talking about race and its part in perpetuating the negative feelings different people feel for one another. It remains to be seen if he will lose the support of white voters after his honest assessment of America.

Obama did gain an important supporter not long after delivering his speech. Governor Bill Richardson of New Mexico is the only Hispanic governor in the nation, and Clinton and Obama had been working for months to get his vote. (He is a superdelegate.) Once the U.S. Ambassador to the United Nations, Richardson had even worked in President Bill Clinton's cabinet as secretary of the U.S. Department of Energy. Therefore, many people expected him to back Hillary Clinton. But as those in politics tried to drive a wedge between black voters and Hispanic voters, claiming that there was animosity and competition between the two groups, Richardson's endorsement after Obama's speech made it clear that these two prominent Americans were working to move past race and live up to the promise of this country as being the land of opportunity for all.

If you're wondering in your heart
whether this country really has the capacity
to rise above its divisions,
look to the title of this book.

Barack Obama's parents—
both of them—
would be proud.

"... But in the unlikely story
            that is America,
there has never been anything
        false about hope.
For when we have faced down
                    impossible odds,
        when we've been told that
we're not ready, or that we
shouldn't try, or that we can't,
            generations of Americans
        have responded
with a simple creed that sums up
        the spirit of a people.

                Yes we can."[29]

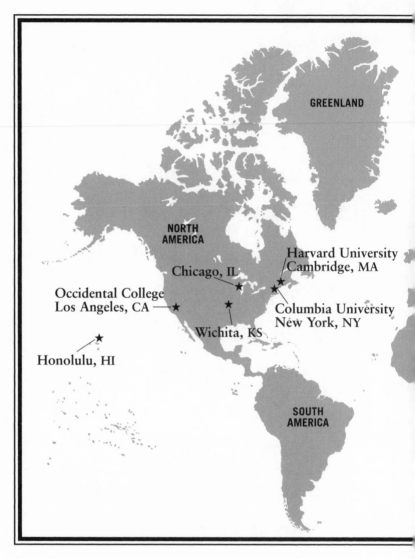

GREENLAND

NORTH
AMERICA

Harvard University
Cambridge, MA

Chicago, IL

Occidental College
Los Angeles, CA

Columbia University
New York, NY

Wichita, KS

Honolulu, HI

SOUTH
AMERICA

Barack Obama is a citizen of the world. His father was born in Kenya; his mother was born in Kansas. Barack was born in Hawaii, moved to Indonesia as a child, and then moved back to Hawaii to finish middle school and high school. He attended college, graduate school, and law

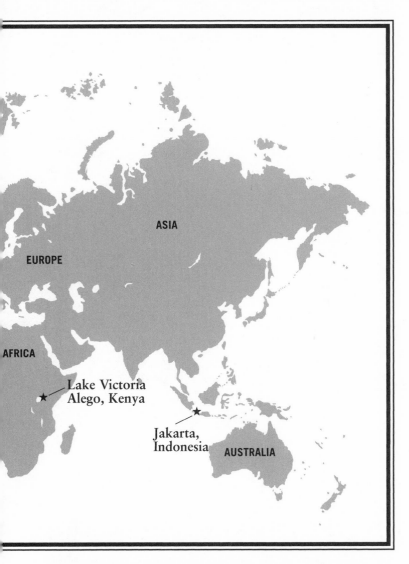

ASIA

EUROPE

AFRICA

Lake Victoria
Alego, Kenya

Jakarta,
Indonesia   AUSTRALIA

school in California, New York, Massachusetts, and Illinois. In 1985, before starting law school at Harvard, Barack traveled to Kenya for the first time to meet his father's family.

BIBLIOGRAPHY

Many sources were scoured to create this biography, an in-depth study of Barack Obama's pursuit of his past and reclamation of his future. Obama's own memoir, *Dreams from My Father*, gives a detailed account of his childhood and search for identity, from which many of the episodes related here were drawn. Efforts were made to uncover the real identities of those named in that work and shield the identities of those who wished to remain anonymous. Another very helpful resource was David Mendell's *Obama: From Promise to Power*, which is filled with first-person accounts and interviews of those who knew Barack when. The information culled from all the works listed below was digested and reborn as the work you have read today.

Alexander, George, Derek T. Dingle, Nicole Marie Richardson. "Why Barack Obama Should Be President." *Black Enterprise.* January 2008: 75–80.

Bowers, Bernice. Phone interview.

Brill, Marlene Targ. *Barack Obama: Working to Make a Difference.* Minneapolis: Millbrook Press, 2006.

"Brown University Coach Is Barack Obama's Brother-in-Law." Alison King Interview with Craig Robinson. New England Cable News Web Site. February 29, 2008 <http://www.necn.com/Boston/Poli tics/Brown-University-coach-is-Barack-Obamas-brotherinlaw/ 1204253615.html>

Creagh, Sunanda. "Many Indonesians Cheer Obama in Democrat Race." Reuters. February 6, 2008 <http://www.reuters.com/article/politics-News/idUSJAK18320020080206>

Dougherty, Steve. *Hopes and Dreams: The Story of Barack Obama.* New York: Black Dog & Leventhal Publishers Inc., 2007.

Finnegan, William. "The Candidate: How the Son of a Kenyan Econo-mist Became an Illinois Everyman." *The New Yorker.* May 31, 2004 <http://www.newyorker.com/archive/2004/05/31/040531fa_fact1>

Fouhy, Beth. "Bill Clinton Rejects Criticism Over Race." Associated Press. March 17, 2008 <http://ap.google.com/article/ALeqM5guS jALNYKtc5Nz4EbkuHyQUNSI6gD8VFG80O0>

Harrison, Maureen and Steve Gilbert, eds. *Barack Obama: Speeches 2002–2006.* Carlsbad: Excellent Books, 2007.

Healy, Patrick. "Clinton Steals Obama's Fund-Raising Thunder." *New York Times.* October 3, 2007 <http://www.nytimes.com/2007/10/03/ us/politics/03campaign.html?_r=1&ref=todayspaper&oref=slogin>

Heilemann, John. "Money Chooses Sides." *New York.* April 23, 2007: 42–121. <http://nymag.com/news/politics/30634/>

Hofmann, Deborah. "Best Sellers: A Different Type of Ranking." *New York Times.* February 16, 2008 <http://query.nytimes.com/gst/full-page.html?res=9F0CE1DE153CF935A25751C0A96E9C8B63>

Kakutani, Michiko. "Obama's Foursquare Politics, with a Dab of Dijon." *New York Times.* October 17, 2006 <http://www.nytimes.com/2006/ 10/17/books/17kaku.html>

Kantor, Jodi. "In Law School, Obama Found Political Voice." *New York Times.* January 28, 2007 <http://www.nytimes.com/2007/01/28/us/ politics/28obama.html?scp=1&sq=%22in+law+school+obama+foun d+political+voice%22&st=nyt>

Kennedy, Caroline. "A President Like My Father." *New York Times.* January 27, 2008 <http://www.nytimes.com/2008/01/27/opinion/ 27kennedy.html>

Klein, Joe. "Why Barack Obama Could Be the Next President." *Time.* October 23, 2006: 45–49.

Kleine, Ted. "Is Bobby Rush in Trouble?: Two Formidable Opponents in the Race for His Congressional Seat Are Banking on It." *Chicago Reader.* March 17, 2000 <http://www.chicagoreader.com/obama/ 000317/>

Korb, Lawrence and Ian Moss. "Factor Military Duty into Criticism." *Chicago Tribune.* April 3, 2008 <http://www.chicagotribune.com/ news/chi-oped0404wrightapr03,0,92000.story>

Kornreich, Lauren, Mark Preston and Paul Steinhauser. "Clinton Outpaces Obama in Fundraising for Third Quarter." CNN Web Site. October 2, 2007 <http://www.cnn.com/2007/POLITICS/10/02/campaign.cash/>

Levenson, Michael and Jonathan Saltzman. "At Harvard Law, a Unifying Voice." *The Boston Globe.* January 28, 2007 <http://www.bostonglob .com/news/local/articles/2007/01/28/at_harvard_law_a_unifying_ voice/?page/1>

Loui, Ronald P. E-mail conversations/interview

McCauley, Gina. "Jesse Jackson: Jesse Jackson on the South Carolina Primary." *Essence.* January 28, 2008 <http://www.essence.com/ essence/lifestyle/voices/0,16109,1706948,00.html>

McCormick, John, Mike Dorning and Jill Zuckman. "Obama Fundraising Rivals Clinton." *Chicago Tribune.* April 5, 2007 <http://www .chicagotribune.com/news/politics/chi-070404obama-money,0, 7560926.story>

Mendell, David. *Obama: From Promise to Power.* New York: Amistad (HarperCollins), 2007.

Obama, Barack. *The Audacity of Hope: Thoughts on Reclaiming the American Dream.* New York: Crown Publishers, 2006.

Obama, Barack. *Dreams from My Father: A Story of Race and Inheritance.* New York: Times Books, 1995.

"Obama Placed Under Secret Service Protection." NBC News and News Services and the Associated Press. May 3, 2007 <http://www. msnbc.msn.com/id/18474444/>

Robinson, Mike. "Obama Got Start in Civil Rights Practice." Associated Press. February 20, 2007 <http://www.boston.com/news/nation/ articles/2007/02/20/obama_got_start_in_civil_rights_practice/>

Sabarini, Prodita. "Indonesia: Impish Obama Couldn't Sit Still, Says School Pal: School That Presidential Hopeful Attended Refutes U.S. Media Reports That It Is a Madrassa." *The Jakarta Post.* January 31, 2007 <http://www.asiamedia.ucla.edu/article-southeastasia. asp?parentid=62743>

Schamberg, Kirsten and Kim Barker. "The Not-So-Simple Story of Barack Obama's Youth." *Chicago Tribune.* March 25, 2007 <http:// www.chicagotribune.com/news/politics/chi=0703250359mar25,1,61 24597.story?page/4&coll/chi=news=hed>

Schuman, Michael A. *Barack Obama: "We Are One People."* Berkeley Heights, NJ: Enslow Publishers, Inc., 2008.

Scott, Janny. "A Free-Spirited Wanderer Who Set Obama's Path." *New York Times.* March 14, 2008 <http://www.nytimes.com/2008/ 03/14/ us/politics/14obama.html?pagewanted=1&hp>

Seelye, Katharine Q. and Julie Bosman. "Ferraro's Obama Remarks Become Talk of Campaign." *New York Times.* March 12, 2008 <http:// www.nytimes.com/2008/03/12/us/politics/12campaign. html?ref=politics>

Tapper, Jake. "Life of Obama's Childhood Friend Takes Drastically Different Path: Story of Keith Kakugawa Provides Interesting Window Into Life of Obama." ABC News Web Site. March 30, 2007 <http:// abcnews.go.com/GMA/story?id=2989722&page=1>

Tapper, Jake. "Nothing Extreme About Indonesian School Attended by Obama: ABC News Visits School in Jakarta, Indonesia, That Has Caused Furor Around Presidential Hopeful." ABC News Web Site. January 25, 2007 <http://abcnews.go.com/Politics/Story?id=2822061 &page=3>

Watson, Paul. "Islam an Unknown Factor in Obama Bid: Campaign Downplays His Connection During Boyhood in Indonesia." *The Baltimore Sun.* March 16, 2007 <http://www.latimes.com/news/nation world/nation/bal-te.obama16mar16,1,7181735,full.story?coll= la-headlines-nation>

Wolffe, Richard and Daren Briscoe. "Across the Divide." *Newsweek.* July 16, 2007: 22–34.

HELPFUL WEB SITES

(relevant articles and information existed at these Web addresses at the time of this book's publication):

http://americanresearchgroup.com/

http://www.barackobama.com

http://www.barackobama.com/2007/02/19/just_because_someone_ writes_it.php

http://www.bnl.gov/bnlweb/pubaf/pr/1998/whpr061898.html

http://www.college.columbia.edu/cct/jan05/cover.php

http://genealogy.about.com/od/aframertrees/p/barack_obama.htm

http://obama.senate.gov

http://www.pbs.org/wnet/aaworld/reference/articles/jesse_jackson.html

http://politics.nytimes.com/election-guide/2008/results/demmap/

http://www.punahou.edu/index.cfm

http://www.punahou.edu/page.cfm?p=601

http://www.salon.com/politics/war_room/index.html

http://www.suntimes.com/images/cds/special/family_tree.html

APPENDIX OF

QUOTATIONS BY

BARACK OBAMA, JR.

INDEX

PHOTO CREDITS